Relaxation

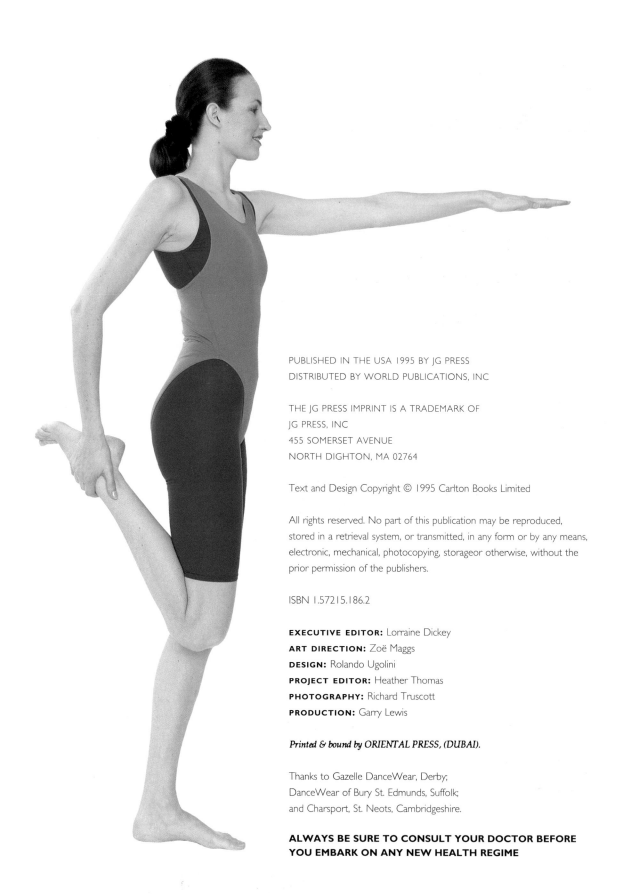

PUBLISHED IN THE USA 1995 BY JG PRESS
DISTRIBUTED BY WORLD PUBLICATIONS, INC

THE JG PRESS IMPRINT IS A TRADEMARK OF
JG PRESS, INC
455 SOMERSET AVENUE
NORTH DIGHTON, MA 02764

ISBN 1.57215.186.2

EXECUTIVE EDITOR: Lorraine Dickey
ART DIRECTION: Zoë Maggs
DESIGN: Rolando Ugolini
PROJECT EDITOR: Heather Thomas
PHOTOGRAPHY: Richard Truscott
PRODUCTION: Garry Lewis

Printed & bound by ORIENTAL PRESS, (DUBAI).

Thanks to Gazelle DanceWear, Derby;
DanceWear of Bury St. Edmunds, Suffolk;
and Charsport, St. Neots, Cambridgeshire.

**ALWAYS BE SURE TO CONSULT YOUR DOCTOR BEFORE
YOU EMBARK ON ANY NEW HEALTH REGIME**

Relaxation

An illustrated program of exercises, techniques and meditations

CHRISSIE GALLAGHER-MUNDY

CONSULTANT EDITOR

NITYA LACROIX

JG PRESS

Contents

Introduction by Nitya Lacroix

Relaxation is a quality of being rather than a state of activity or inactivity. Whether you are busy doing something or you are at rest, true relaxation occurs only when your body and mind are functioning in harmony as an integrated unity, whole and unfragmented.

This delicate relationship of mental and physical equilibrium can be disturbed easily, especially under the toll of modern-day stress. This can mean that even as you try to unwind from the day's events, and attempt to let go of stressful thoughts, your body may still be carrying the residue of accumulated tensions which will deeply affect your ability to relax. Even if you make a special effort to release your physical tensions, such as going for a walk or receiving a massage, if your mind is preoccupied with worries or negative thoughts, then a part of you will remain entangled in the vicious cycle of stress. What is happening to you mentally will determine the health of your physical wellbeing, and how you use your body will profoundly affect your peace of mind.

It is very easy for any of us to sacrifice one aspect of ourselves in order to promote another. If you have an important deadline to meet at work, or a responsibility which cannot be shirked, it may be very tempting to ignore your physical health while trying to meet the demands of the task in hand. If this becomes a pattern of behaviour, then your attempts to relax can be equally frantic, becoming more like a plaster to glue yourself back together

rather than a genuine commitment to healing.

The art of relaxation then is for you to find a way to allow your body and mind to become friends and allies in the face of stress. They need to become equal partners, supporting each other and working together to prevent or redress the imbalances which can occur so easily. This may require developing a whole new awareness of how you can nourish yourself physically, mentally and emotionally so that you can approach your tasks and fulfil your duties with a positive attitude, vigour and enthusiasm. At the same time you need to be able to recognise the signs of stress as they occur, and take the necessary steps to discharge those tensions and replenish your inner resources.

Creating for yourself a healthy, wholesome lifestyle does require adopting a holistic attitude to relaxation. Once you have understood the integral link between your body and mind, you will experience for yourself how emotional stress can cause the muscles in your body to tighten, and that this, in turn, may give you a headache or create lethargy and consequently affect your mental alertness and decision-making abilities. Similarly, a continuous negative thought about yourself or others may lower your self-esteem, causing you to tighten and contract in your body, hunch your shoulders or reduce your breathing as a form of self-protection or as a way to numb your feelings. This, in turn, will inhibit your capacity to be spontaneous, diminishing your ability to respond to the pleasures and joys of life and thus creating a situation for emotional upset. Then, once again, the psychosomatic cycle can begin to turn around on itself.

That is why this book, simply but aptly titled *Relaxation,* is the perfect guide to helping you to achieve a healthy, balanced lifestyle. Chrissie Gallagher-Mundy has provided the reader with many useful tips and exercises which clearly acknowledge the important relationship between body and mind. The book helps you to recognise your own stress levels with its use of easy-to-follow questionnaires. Armed with this awareness, you can then work your way through the book, or pick and choose the programmes most suited to your needs.

This book will help you to understand the causes of stress and how it physically affects your nervous system. While recognising that stress is an inevitable and sometimes essential part of life, Chrissie carefully shows you the way to discharge its harmful side-effects which lodge in your body and mind and diminish your vitality and happiness. Even better, she shows you how to adapt and deal with stress situations in such a way that you can regard them in a positive light. By following the suggestions in this book, and allowing them to become more integral to your activity and recreation, relaxation can become more a way of life than just an antidote to stress.

Chrissie has taken a lively and holistic approach to the subject of relaxation, combining physical and psychological approaches to help you prevent or break out of your tension patterns or to dissolve the unpleasant symptoms of stress once they have become lodged in your body and mind. Full of playful suggestions, as well as careful instruction, this book will help you to achieve a sense of balance and relaxation at home and at work.

In *Relaxation,* you will find many ways to combat simultaneously both psychological and physical stress. While learning how to focus your mind on the immediate job in front of you, you can also become more conscious of your posture and breathing, allowing your body to relax and be revitalized so that your concentration will become even more acute. By taking care of your diet, you will feel more alive in both body and mind. By learning how to take more conscious control over your life, you will feel more in charge of events and this will instill within you a greater feeling of confidence.

Relaxation is a book to inspire you. It will help you to adopt a fresh new approach to your mental and physical wellbeing, and enable you to create a positive attitude to changing old habits which reinforce stress. While it urges you to enrich yourself by making a commitment to a relaxed and healthy lifestyle, it makes the process so much fun that the invitation is hard to refuse.

NITYA LACROIX

Nitya Lacroi

Overcoming stress

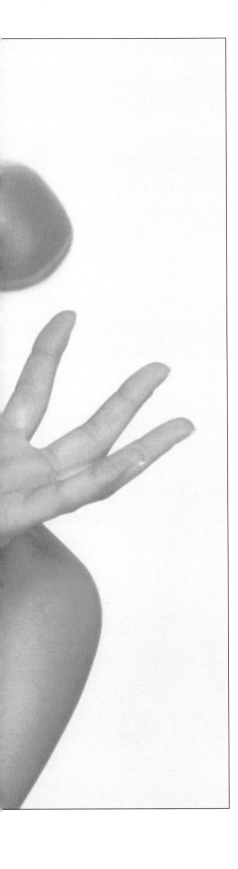

chapter one

THERE HAVE BEEN numerous articles and books written about stress, so much so that it has become a byword in our society. Everybody has heard of the concept of stress but most people do not apply it directly to themselves. It is something that happens to other people; they associate the word with work, pressure from tight deadlines and long working hours. However, stress really means two things: it is a way of describing the challenges that meet us in everyday living and is also the way in which we deal with them. Therefore stress isn't necessarily a bad thing and it is something that we all experience at some time in our lives. Nor is it a phenomenon experienced only by working people; someone who is under-stimulated is just as likely to suffer stressful symptoms as someone who is constantly overworked if personal resources are not there to cope with the situation.

Symptoms and causes

Challenges, then, are options requiring a response or action of some kind, and it is how we react and deal with these that dictates whether the effect on us as individuals is positive or negative. If the challenges are too complicated, then this can create an imbalance between demands and resources and a feeling of pressure, which ultimately gives rise to stressful symptoms.

Stress, positively speaking, is what motivates us and pushes us towards action (termed 'eu-stress'). Some projects may be hard work but we enjoy meeting the challenges they offer to us; for example, bringing up children is taxing yet has its rewards, or there are some deadlines which we can enjoy meeting. These are positive ways of regarding stress. Yet tip the balance a little too far one way and the mother who was happy juggling a busy career and babycare can suffer from 'hurry sickness', a feeling that there's not enough time to do anything satisfactorily. This is an all too commonly felt form of stress where the demands are too much for the time allotted for their accomplishment.

Sometimes there are just too many demands on our time and emotions, and if the actions we respond with are inappropriate or unsatisfactory, then pressure, once again, begins to build (termed 'de-stress   The trouble with pressure is that it is explosive if not dealt with quickly and effectively. It affects us both physically and mentally: in the body this means a variety of physical symptoms can start to occur, such as headaches and irritability, while, mentally, a person becomes edgy and anxious to the point that even the postal delivery being five minutes late can cause distress!

The effects of negative stress have far-reaching effects that go well beyond the individual. In the UK alone, they are said to cost industry anywhere between £40 million and £1.3 billion per year along with claims that over half of the deaths in Great Britain are due to stress-related illness. Stress results in many physical and mental changes in the body all of which add up to, as Dr Hans Seyle puts it, "the rate of wear and tear on the body". If in earlier societies the wear and tear on the body was wrought by mainly physical hardships, such as man-eating animals, having to hunt for food and so on, today's lifestyle has its own combination of physical and mental strains which are just as lethal!

THE PHYSICAL ASPECT

All kinds of situations can cause stress-related symptoms, which is why recognising your own specific stress factors and learning how to cope with them is very important for your relaxation and good health. One of the major problems with modern life in relation to stress results from us being less physically active than our ancestors. Our occupations and lifestyle have become increasingly sophisticated, yet our bodies have not evolved in the same way and still react on a very basic level, and our physical powers are seldom needed for coping

DO YOU SUFFER FROM STRESS?

As already stated, stress isn't just about the pressures in your life but also how you react to and cope with them. Answer the questions below and estimate your stress potential.

		Yes	No
1	Is your sleep erratic or disturbed ?	☐	☐
2	Do you bite your nails or have other nervous tics?	☐	☐
3	Do you want public recognition for things you do?	☐	☐
4	Do you cry or feel like crying often?	☐	☐
5	Do you have difficulty making up your mind or taking decisions?	☐	☐
6	Do you feel unable to cope a lot of the time?	☐	☐
7	Are you constantly irritable and snappy with those close to you?	☐	☐
8	Do you feel a failure ?	☐	☐
9	Do you have disturbing thoughts or fantasies?	☐	☐
10	Do you worry too much over something that is, in fact, unimportant?	☐	☐
11	Are you angered easily by events and people?	☐	☐
12	Are you impatient with any delays?	☐	☐
13	Do you dislike yourself?	☐	☐
14	Do you feel dissatisfied with yourself or your life?	☐	☐
15	Do you feel nauseous, faint or sweat for no obvious reason?	☐	☐

If the answer to the majority of these questions is "yes", you could probably benefit from some relaxation techniques as outlined later in this book. Most of the situations mentioned in the questions above are centred within your personality. Yet it is possible to consciously change your stress reactions.

Now answer these questions to see how you are affected in a stressful situation.

		Yes	No
1	Are you tense? Do your shoulders and neck feel tight and stiff?	☐	☐
2	Do you lie awake at night worrying and planning the next day?	☐	☐
3	Are you smoking or drinking more than usual?	☐	☐
4	Are you eating less or less well than usual?	☐	☐
5	Do you feel guilty when relaxing and not doing things?	☐	☐
6	Do you start one task before you have finished another?	☐	☐
7	Do you experience a dry mouth or sweaty palms?	☐	☐
8	Do you find yourself snapping or yelling at people in the car or in a shop?	☐	☐
9	Do you feel you have too much to think about and too much to cope with?	☐	☐
10	Do you feel frequently frustrated and let down by other people?	☐	☐
11	Do you have ringing in the ears or other head noises?	☐	☐
12	Do you seem to get any illness that is around?	☐	☐
13	Do you have difficulties in thinking about and solving problems?	☐	☐
14	Do you get recurring headaches or other recurring physical symptoms?	☐	☐
15	Do you feel fine until one small incident like the car not starting makes your whole life seem unmanageable?	☐	☐

Again, if you answered "yes" to more than half of these questions, this book may help you to take steps to reduce your stress condition.

with stress. Driving to the supermarket and doing the weekly shop is a fairly mundane activity yet finding food for the family once presented the ultimate physical and mental adventure! Most working environments used to be physically demanding but now, with the growth of technology, many jobs have been reduced to the minimal operating of machinery or a sedentary posture for much of the day. Thus physical challenges are disappearing as ever more mental challenges present themselves.

Physical changes take place in response to all stresses and strains, and anything perceived as a threat causes the body to prepare itself for appropriate physical action in the form of fight or flight (see page 20). Thus we develop tension of both 'thought and musculature' which usually is not put to good use and stays in the body, causing problems. Experts predict we will be well into the twenty first century before man's responses and defences adapt to modern life.

What happens when the body is under stress? When pressure builds up the body gears itself for action and this involves a series of physiological changes. First the body is readied for action: the blood supply is increased to the brain and also to the muscles, which are tense in anticipation of activity. To facilitate this, the blood supply is diverted from other areas, such as the kidneys and sexual organs, while the intestines and stomach are put on hold. The pituitary gland is activated and hence the production of adrenalin and noradrenalin. This, in turn, triggers further changes. The pupils dilate (to see better), the heart beats more strongly and the lungs take in air more quickly to oxygenate the blood. The liver metabolizes fats and stored glucose in preparation for the extra energy needed, and the bowel and bladder functions are speeded up. The increase in blood supply to already tense muscles means an increase in blood pressure.

Changes like these, unless discharged by physical activity, are bound to take their toll. Your mood changes and you become more serious as you concentrate. As saliva dries up, you experience a dry mouth. With the interruption of digestive functioning you could suffer heartburn and indigestion. As the blood supply to the skin decreases, it can become over-sensitive and give rise to rashes and itching while the speeding up of bowel and bladder may cause an immediate urge to run to the toilet!

While these symptoms are usually only temporary, if the stress situation occurs frequently or becomes a chronic state of affairs, then more long-term drawbacks may start to occur. This is where the body starts to make alterations for its constant state of arousal and is known as the General Adaptation Syndrome. The increase of blood to the brain can cause headaches and even migraine, while increased flow to muscles that remain tense causes muscle spasm and stiffness. If the chest is pumping continually, then pains and angina can occur, and if the blood is always being directed away from various organs, then ulcers and a lack of sexual response can also lead to problems. Also, if

Opposite: when you have too many different things to handle all at once and cannot focus on one issue at a time, you can become stressed. Many working mothers, trying to juggle a baby and a career, experience this.

the liver is always manically converting glucose and the heart is always pumping over-enthusiastically there is a greater propensity to illnesses such as diabetes or hypertension.

As you can see, stress puts a strain on the system which, if it is not dealt with appropriately, can literally start to wear the body out. Before dealing with the symptoms, however, we have to recognise the reasons and the triggers that cause our bodies to go into overdrive.

ARE YOU A TYPE A OR B PERSONALITY?

Experts now define personalities into two broad types: type **A** and type **B**. Although most of us are a combination of both **A** and **B**, some people definitely exhibit a greater proportion of **A** characteristics than **B**. Look at the list below to decide which you might be.

Either Or

1   Do you enjoy tight deadlines and strive hard to keep them **OR** are you more relaxed about them and unfazed? ☐ ☐

2   Do you find that you are on the go all the time and seldom sit down to read or listen to the radio **OR** do you make some time in your day for switching off and relaxing? ☐ ☐

3   Do you take on many different tasks at once, sometimes before finishing your original work **OR** do you tend to let your work schedules slide from time to time, even getting behind with some things? ☐ ☐

4   Do you find yourself becoming impatient when others are slower than you **OR** do you not notice whether people are fast or slow? ☐ ☐

5   Do you find yourself doing two or three things at once, e.g. making telephone calls while watching **TV** or flicking through a magazine while you listen to the radio **OR** do you get quite drowsy in the evening? ☐ ☐

6   Do you eat standing up or while doing something else **OR** do you forget to eat at all? ☐ ☐

TYPE A PERSONALITY

If you answered "yes" to the first part of the majority of questions then the chances are that you are a Type **A** personality. This has its advantages; for example, **A** types tend to be stubborn and persist until they get things done. They also work hard and achieve where others may fail.

If you can identify with these Type **A** characteristics, you need to be aware that you may be prone to doing things too quickly. Why not try making relaxation part of your daily routine to combat any negative effects of your busy lifestyle?

TYPE B PERSONALITY

If you answered "yes" to the second part of the majority of questions, then you are probably a Type **B**. This means that you may suffer less from stress brought on yourself by tight deadlines, too many jobs etc., but you may still be prone to outside stresses, or even negative stress due to things not happening in your life.

Try to evaluate your **A** and **B** characteristics and find a balance between them so that you are motivated about things that matter, and can relax about other things.

MENTAL FACTORS

The causes of stress obviously vary from person to person and what factor makes one person worry might not trouble someone else. Nevertheless, there are fundamental changes that occur in most people's lives and which are generally accepted as difficult to deal with and are therefore potentially stressful. The death of a loved one, divorce, moving jobs, houses and out of your neighbourhood are all rated highly as very stressful events. Then there are less traumatic ones such as family quarrels, trouble at work or disagreements with friends, or a change in social or work routine.

In addition, there are further everyday problems which, over a period of time, accumulate to cause a powerful stress reaction. Life is for ever changing and the social structure upon which we base our lives is becoming ever more complicated and demanding. Educational methods are changing so fast that by the time many teenagers leave school what they have learned will already be out of date! Learning is also far removed from their parents' school days, which widens the generation gap even further and can cause problems in the family.

Technology evolves so fast that by the time one piece of equipment is purchased another more sophisticated model may be required. Advertising continually pressurizes us to want and purchase more which requires higher earnings and longer hours spent working away from home. The break up of the family unit due to all kinds of pressures has been a major concern for some time now.

Even in what used to be regarded as non-work time, such as travelling on trains or planes, with the advent of computers, mobile phones and other new technology we can even work while en route to and from the office as well as when we actually get there!

Our minds have also developed to the extent that we now start to anticipate problems before they even occur. By virtue of world-wide communications, we can understand and worry about global problems and catastrophes in other countries, as well as our own personal problems, such as the behaviour of our colleagues, illness in the family and whether we can afford a holiday this year.

Some people are more affected by problems than others, and our attitudes and personal beliefs also make a difference to how we perceive problems. If we pressurize ourselves to achieve more than is possible, then feelings of self-doubt and disappointment emerge. If we indulge in 'if only' behaviour, coveting lifestyles and circumstances that are not available to us, then discontentment soon starts to build. In this way, uncertainty and insecurity may lead to poor self-esteem and we end up looking and feeling worried all the time! While many of our problems, both at work and at home, and pressures are outside of our control, this is not the case with the way we feel due to the beliefs we hold. For instance, be assured that all of us, no matter what our position in society, wealth and status, are only human and fallible.

Dealing with stress

The best way of dealing with stress is first to learn to recognise it and then to try and understand what triggers it off for you. Only then can you begin to practise some stress avoidance and learn the best ways of handling it. Tackling stress needs a holistic approach in which all mental, physical and emotional aspects of your life need to be examined.

A MENTAL APPROACH

Some people are better copers, even in worse circumstances, than others. Whether you are a type A or B personality has some bearing on how you cope with stress. Dr Ray of the School of Health Studies at Wolverhampton Polytechnic, England, also talks of slow and fast 'recoverers'. While acknowledging that everybody suffers some stress, he makes the point that whereas for some people it is just a temporary annoyance, for others it becomes a much more prolonged situation. People who hold grudges, for instance, are more likely to be slow recoverers. Rather than letting go of an unpleasant situation, they hold on to the bad feelings which only serves to upset themselves more. 'If only' behaviour can also be self-destructive: unfulfilled expectations often lead to fretting while always looking to the future will not solve today's problems. The best way is to try to live in the present, accepting the limitations of your position and looking to the past neither with remorse nor nostalgia. Instead, you should learn from the experiences of the past and laugh. Try to look to the future as an opportunity to embrace new experiences.

Remember that negative feelings can be replaced by positive ones. The same situation can look totally different when viewed from two different perspectives. Although many of the stressors in everyday life are beyond your physical control, you can change your mental responses to them and this can make all the difference. Try not to waste mental energy on things you can't change. For instance, if your neighbours are noisy do what you can about it: talk to them, talk to your local authority or even consider moving. However, when you have done all the physical things focus your mind elsewhere and try not to dwell on it. Don't let it become an obsession; instead you could try out some practical measures like wearing ear plugs at night, or practising the relaxation and visualization techniques suggested in this book.

In the same way, you can try to modify your response towards people you find annoying. Each time you react the same way you are reinforcing a negative pattern and distressing yourself. Try to state your case clearly and simply, make sure you have your say but be prepared to listen to the other person – really listen! Imagine if they felt the same way about you – you would want them to listen! Interaction is so much more fruitful. You could be pleasantly surprised! After all, it's only you who stands to gain. Learn to recognise your own personality traits; often it is easier to recognise them in others, maybe even in the people you dislike! A lot of what irritates us about our own families are the personality traits we have ourselves! Finally, learn to reprogramme your reactions with the exercise in the box (right).

CONFIDENCE

Try to be realistic about your expectations for yourself and also to judge whether other people's expectations of you are realistic. Use your imagination as a positive force; imagine only positive outcomes, rehearse only scenes of success in your mind and look on the bright side! You might as well! You lose nothing by being cheerful and it gives you a lively appearance to which the world responds. Looking and appearing light-hearted will help you to acquire self-confidence. Everyone suffers periods of uncertainty over specific situations from time to time. Self-confidence really develops from a feeling that you have some degree of control over your life events (as much as anyone can). This then frees you to get involved in the lives and society of others so you become less self-obsessed. Then you can view life's vicissitudes as an exciting challenge rather than as a threat.

A PRACTICAL APPROACH

A healthy body with a healthy immune system helps us cope with stress. Physically there are many ways to try and combat stress or avoid its symptoms. Some will be dealt with in more detail later on in this book; others are mentioned below.

Slowing down can help focus your attention on

COPING WITH STRESSFUL SITUATIONS

1 List all the situations that make you stressed.
2 List them in order of how much stress they cause you.
3 Now list them in order of how important those things really are to you.
4 Study the different orders of the two lists to help you to become aware of how you can become stressed over relatively unimportant issues.
5 Now use the situations (particularly the most unimportant ones) to combat stress: Remember your stress situations and when they start to happen. Use them as a cue to relax. When you are stuck in traffic use that to remind you to stretch out any tense muscles (see page 22). When your boss or work colleagues wind you up, do some breathing exercises (see page 66). Try smiling at someone when you feel like shouting at someone else! In this way you will be turning the tables on your stressors and using them to your benefit!

the task in hand rather than tearing around trying to accomplish three things at once. Work on one thing at a time and concentrate on how you are doing the task; enjoy the work in progress rather than just looking towards the finish. Concentrate on the means rather than the end. It was Sir Thomas More, the sixteenth-century English humanist, who always insisted that he gave complete concentration to whatever task he was engaged in, large or small. Try it, and you will find you waste less energy, cut down tensions and barriers and, ultimately, accomplish things quicker. Don't waste energy on things that are unimportant. Instead, try to conserve your energy and pace yourself.

Physical stress routines

You may be surprised to learn that an effective mental and physical exercise for relieving stress is juggling! It can help you to concentrate your mind and body on a single task. If you practise juggling with balls for just twenty minutes you will soon start to make progress. Juggling involves hand-eye co-ordination as well as mind-body co-ordination. It is this kind of activity that brings the whole body and mind together and focuses it, thereby obliterating other thoughts and worries. It uses the mind for skill and co-ordination, and the body's dexterity and flexibility. It's also a great way of getting yourself moving and increasing your level of physical activity!

Juggling exercise

Start by standing up straight with three soft juggling balls at your feet. Pick two of the three balls up and hold one in each hand. Stand up straight with shoulders relaxed and elbows tucked into the waist, so that the forearms are parallel with the floor and palms are facing upwards with a ball nestling comfortably in each one. When you throw, use the lower arms; do not extend the whole arm away from your body.

Stage one

1   Throw one ball in to the air at a time and catch it. When you throw, try to ensure that the throw is absolutely vertical so that you open your hand and the ball drops right back into the palm. Don't throw the ball any higher than eye level so that your gaze can remain steady and your head is not thrown back. Repeat with both hands until you have a smooth confident motion.

2   Try the same action whilst throwing both balls into the air at the same time and then catching them simultaneously. Don't let the fact that you are now having to throw two balls rather than one make you lose control. Progress slowly and surely and calmly. Make sure both throws are vertical and steady and at the same speed.

3   Take just one ball in one hand and throw it so that it describes an arc in the air. Thus the ball leaves one hand and arcs into its high point level with the middle of your forehead or just above, and

controlled. The rhythm is: "Throw 1, Throw 2, Catch 1, Catch 2". Simple!

2 As before, you are still throwing the balls in sequence but now you must cross them in the air. To do this, the first and second balls must describe an arc with the high point level with the middle of your forehead. Again, the bottom of the arc is the hands throwing and catching on either side.

So throw ball 1 in an arc, throw ball 2, catch ball 1, then catch ball 2. Both balls should have described the same arc in the air, reaching the same high point (level with the forehead) and dropping into the opposite hand. Practise this for a while until you are confident.

Stage three

Now for the real test of your control! Pick up all three balls. Hold two in your right hand and one in your left. You are going to add the third ball into the sequence. If you have practised well, then adding the third ball is purely logical, but again it takes mind over matter to make the body perform what the brain knows it needs to do.

So throw ball 1 (in right hand) into its arc, throw ball 2 from the left hand. Catch ball 1. Throw ball 3 from the right hand in order to catch ball 2. Throw ball 1 again in order to catch ball 3!

This may sound terribly complicated but once you have a go it all falls into place and you develop a rhythm! What you have to concentrate on is throwing the balls. Too many people try and hold on to the balls so that they end up with two balls in one hand. There is only ever one ball in each hand and the other ball is in the air.

then curves down into your waiting palm on the other side. Practise this move until it is smooth and unhurried. Keep the elbow tucked in so that the arms are not flailing all over the place and keep the eye level steady and to the front.

Practise these three steps until they are smooth and you can perform them with a relaxed gaze to the front.

Stage two

This stage is a lot harder because it involves throwing the two balls in sequence.

1 Holding one ball in each hand, throw the first ball into the air, then throw the second ball into the air. Now catch the first one (in the same hand that threw it) and then catch the second in the second hand. Make sure the height of the throws is still at eye level or just above and that they are vertical and

FRUSTRATION ROUTINE

When frustration and difficulties start to accumulate over the course of a day, tension begins to build in the body, both internally and externally. Certain muscles begin to tighten and your breathing becomes more rapid or held. This is known as the 'fight or flight' syndrome; it is when the brain perceives danger and to preserve itself the body gets ready to fight or run. Unfortunately, in modern living, the situations that cause these responses are not ones that can be solved either by running away or fighting!

In the privacy of your own home, however, it can often help to let off steam by doing something physical. Spend a few minutes doing this simple explosive routine and put those fighting muscles into action to get rid of all that pent-up tension!

Use this physical dance routine as a focus for your feelings, turning what you are feeling into movement. Punch the air and thrust your arms very aggressively if you are feeling angry. Try doing it more slowly and fluidly if you are feeling sad. Use the sadness to change the movement into something more undulating or subtle if that is what the sadness makes you feel. In this way, you are using your body to relieve the mental tension within you, and one part of the body can help to heal another. Try this routine particularly if you are frustrated, when you feel cornered or unable to resolve a situation. Many people who have been imprisoned cite

FRUSTRATION ROUTINE

1   **Stand with feet apart, hands by your sides. Extend the right arm out forcefully, reaching across the chest as if reaching out to someone.**

2   **Step forwards on your left foot and pull your right arm in towards the solar plexus, sharply curling over as you do so – as if someone has punched you in the stomach.**

    Repeat steps 2 and 3 on the other side for two more counts. Try to feel that as you curl over you are scooping out the negative energy. As you extend the arm, imagine that you're throwing all that energy and tension away beyond the finger tips.

3   **Punch upwards with the right arm, fist clenched, to the left diagonal. Now punch outwards along the right diagonal with the left arm.**

4   **Drop your head into both arms, covering your eyes with your forearms and bending the knees. Screw up your face as if you are having a good cry, or yell.**

5   **Finally, drop your arms back by your sides and straighten up slowly, lifting your face up to the ceiling. Remain there while you let the tension fall from your face and shoulders, through the torso to the floor. Try this routine to all four corners of the room and try to put different feelings into this routine and see how this changes the movement.**

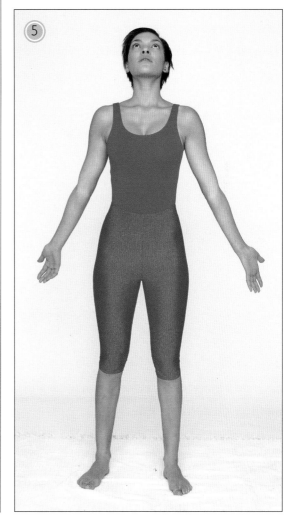

physical exercise as a way of helping them to cope with both the physical and mental pressures.

Doing this routine won't solve all your problems but it will put your fight or flight muscles into action and prevent mental tension building up physically in your body. You might well feel able to deal with your mental challenges with a calmer and clearer mind!

Relieving tension

Another quite different way of dealing with tension is rocking chair therapy! If you have a comfortable chair in which you can sit and rock gently, you can find this very settling and calming after a hard day!

As well as everyday tensions and frustrations, periods of enforced immobility can take their toll on the body. Sitting at a desk or being stuck in a car for long periods can cause stiffness in muscles and joints, even without added frustrations.

If you are stuck in these situations for more than 20 minutes at a time, try to spend five minutes doing these simple exercises. They will stretch and invigorate inactive muscles while helping to promote blood flow to stiff areas.

IN THE CAR

Make sure that you are stationary while doing these exercises!

1   Stretch both arms up to the roof of your car. Walk your arms back a few paces so that you are stretching your shoulder joints. At the same time ease your rib cage and chest forwards so as to arch the back slightly. This will release tension across the shoulders and the lower back. Finally, press the lower back into the seat, pulling in on the stomach muscles, and lower the arms.

2   Brace your arms straight, hands on the steering wheel, and press your body deep into the seat while lifting up tall through the waist to elongate the spine. Feel as if your head is pressing upwards towards the roof and your coccyx downwards through the seat, while pressing your shoulder blades together and down, lengthening the neck. Breathe regularly as you press and release; this will help to lengthen and release the spine from its cramped position.

3   Sit up straight and squeeze the muscles at the side of the waist to lift one hip up towards the rib cage; then lift the other hip up to the other side. This flexing of the spine on a different plane will help to loosen up the lower back.

4   Stop what you are doing, look straight ahead, and relax the shoulders and hands for a few seconds. Now begin to lengthen the spine by lifting the rib cage upwards and inwards, pulling in on the abdominals and pushing the top of the head towards the ceiling. Clasp the hands and use them to press the head forwards so that the chin tucks into the chest. Keep the lower spine straight so that the stretch is felt from the base of the skull spreading out across the shoulders. Then release your hands and return your head to an upright position. Repeat this every time you feel tension building in the neck and upper back. Take a deep breath and gently roll the shoulders forwards and backwards to refocus your attention.

Opposite: sit quietly in your favourite chair and just contemplate your day. Let the negative events enter your mind but pass over them quickly. Just focus on the positive accomplishments of the day.

STRETCHES FOR THE OFFICE

Working for long periods at a desk, particularly when staring at a computer screen, can lead eventually to the top of your back beginning to curve. If your chin juts forwards it can make the spine a mass of uncomfortable curves. Break your body's bad habits by stopping work occasionally to run through these quick stretches to restore balance and boost circulation to the brain!

1 Resting your hands by your sides, stretch your neck out by pressing your right ear towards your right shoulder. Slowly bring your head upright and round to the left shoulder. Look as far as you can over the shoulder, then press your ear sideways once more. Repeat to the other side.

2 Sit up straight in your chair and let your head roll forwards, curving the spine with it. Exhale as you let this continue in a smooth motion with the arms falling towards the floor until your chest is resting on your thighs with head relaxed forwards. The lower position of the head will refresh the brain with blood. (Don't stay there too long or you may become dizzy.) Inhale as you slowly roll up through the spine.

3 Sitting squarely on your chair with both buttocks touching the seat, pull up in the abdomen and rib cage, hands by your sides. Now reach one arm down towards the floor pulling the body over into a side stretch. Reach as far as you can without over-balancing. Repeat on the other side. Flexing the spine laterally keeps it mobile and helps prevent

AVOIDING EYE STRAIN

When using computers, or even just concentrating on small print, eye strain can occur and it can help just to relax the eyes and face for a moment. Take time out from your work to let your gaze rest in the distance and your eyes refocus. Then screw up your face, scrunching your eyes and mouth tightly and hold. Keeping the eyes closed, slowly relax the facial muscles registering the tension falling out of each part of the face. Repeat these scrunches three times and then slowly open the eyes and return to concentration.

stiffness. (If your chair has arm rests that prevent you leaning over, put one arm on the arm rest and reach the other arm in the air and up over to the side.)

4 Exercise the eye muscles. Without moving your head, take your eyes as far upwards as they will go.

Don't strain. Now take them to the right and then left. Then look downwards as far as your eyes will allow. Rest. Now try holding up a finger in front of your face and focusing on it, then look at the background, now look at the finger again and, finally, return your focus to the background. You will be using the different muscles of the eye as you change your viewing distance, and relieving the over-use of one line of vision the whole time. You can even buy books and posters that play games with vision, and if you relax your eyes enough you can see new images that are not initially apparent; these books are good exercise for the eyes!

Small breaks like these can help to increase blood flow to areas of the body restricted by tension, and allow you more energy to carry on.

HOME STRETCH

Busy people at home can also benefit from some time out for stretches. When you rush about, up and down stairs, bending and twisting, an overwhelming tiredness can suddenly set in. Stop for five minutes and perform this small routine to help you continue with renewed energy.

These small stretches should be fitted into your daily routine on a regular basis – they will help to prevent tensions building up in the muscle fibres and, thus, stiffness.

1 Realign that spine again. Reach the hands towards the ceiling and, taking a deep breath in, swing the arms down past the ankles with a bend in the knees.

2 Swing back up and, dropping one arm on to the hip, lean into a side bend, keeping both feet firmly on the floor. Repeat to the other side.

① ②

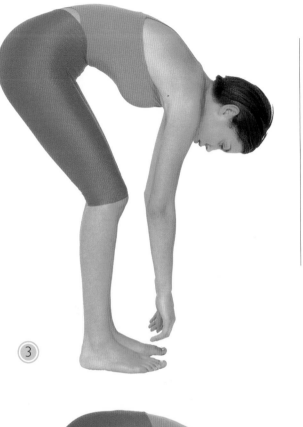

3 From the side bend, take the arm down towards the floor bringing the torso with it, ending with knees bent and head and hands hanging limp towards the floor. Inhale and exhale.

4 Bend the knees until both your hands touch the floor and, keeping the hands there, try to straighten the legs as much as you can.

5 Bend the knees once more and lift up in the stomach. Lifting the head last, roll through the spine to return to the standing position.

Body awareness

chapter two

BECOMING AWARE of your body and its resources is one of the essential ways towards relaxation and healthier living in general. Your body is equipped with vast capabilities to keep you on an even keel and protect you from harm. Learn to listen to your body and respond to its messages as you receive them. The brain constantly absorbs vast amounts of information and sifts through it to bring us the important data we need to know. For instance, when you are playing tennis, there are hundreds of thousands of different messages coming from all your sensory organs to be dealt with and assessed. Think of the hundreds of precisely timed movements that are required to make each passing shot and consider all the value judgements, feelings, experiences and ambitions that accompany each move! Your body has amazing capabilities.

Homeostasis

The body has all kinds of ways to help it maintain its comfortable status quo; this is known as homeostasis. Most people are aware of the body's ability to maintain a reasonable temperature. If you get too hot the body produces fluids to cool the skin, and if you get too cold your hairs are used to trap warm air, while movements (shivering) are produced to raise body temperature. There are countless other devices that maintain your equilibrium: for example, if you climb mountains your body will

SELF-HELP CURES FOR YOU TO TRY

There are some physical conditions that we can do something positive about to prevent them and reduce their effects. For example, when people with Raunauds disease get cold, the arteries in their extremities constrict and reduce blood flow to the fingers or toes to such an extent that they may turn blue or lose all feeling in them. Drug treatments may sometimes have unpleasant side-effects and can cause headaches and reddened skin in other areas. Some doctors recommend visualization, and if you suffer from this, you could try taking a few minutes of each day, as the weather gets colder, and imagine yourself lying on a warm beach. Wave your feet or hands about and imagine them pressing into the warm sand, burrowing deeper and deeper into the warmth. Now picture the vessels in your fingers or toes widening as the warmth of the sun shines down upon them. Start to feel as if your hands and feet are full of warm blood circulating around the digits. With practice this could help return the flow of blood to your hands and feet. Remember to try this every time you start to feel cold.

Varicose veins are another common medical condition that you can help to guard against. If you spend a lot of time standing on your feet, try to find several opportunities during the day to contract your legs, particularly the calf muscles. Do this by lifting your heels and pressing up on the toes as high as you can. Repeat three or four times. Next bend one knee, pressing your heel behind you towards your buttock. Repeat this gently but speedily three or four times. Finally lift one foot off the floor flexing and extending the foot as far each way as you can. These simple exercises will help to keep the blood flowing up the legs.

Migraines are still a medical mystery but they are thought to be partly the body's response to stress. When the body perceives a threat, blood is diverted to the muscles and the supply to the brain is restricted. When the crisis passes the vessels re-open and blood goes surging back to the brain. As with the pain experienced when blood rushes into the fingers after being frozen, the pain of blood flowing back into the brain is intense and is felt as a migraine.

It seems that when blood is constricted towards the brain it also shows itself in constriction in the extremities. So if you can concentrate on diverting the blood into your fingers and toes you will also be pushing blood towards the brain. Use the method described above for Raunauds disease to push the blood towards the hands and feet. If you do this when you feel that a migraine is imminent you may keep the blood flowing towards the brain and thereby prevent restriction and subsequent consequences. While there are other factors involved this could help prevent the pain of a migraine. This also means, of course, listening to your body and noticing the danger signs before the migraine really takes hold.

adjust to the levels of oxygen in the air; and if you stay in the sun for any length of time, melanin (what we perceive as a tan) is produced to protect the skin from further damage. Thus, people from hotter countries tend to be born with darker skins and darker eyes, which are less sensitive to light.

If you injure yourself, in most cases your body can start the repair process before you consult a doctor; cuts heal over and the body even plays doctor and offers its own diagnoses in some circumstances. For example, when certain areas swell after a sprain or injury, this may be a response to prevent harmful movement. Feet and hands often develop hard skin to protect them from wear and tear.

There are circumstances where the body's natural resistance and responses are over-ridden and you may need to seek medical advice. However, it will help you if you can become aware of how your mind can assist your body with its own self-healing. The natural processes in your body can be inhibited by your lifestyle, and if this is the case, you can change things for yourself. For instance, when your circulatory system becomes sluggish due to a sedentary lifestyle, you could try an active approach to boost your blood and lymph flow.

Listen to your body

Noticing danger signs is a very important part of body awareness and can lead to an improvement in both your mental and physical approach to many areas of your life, so listen to your body.

Constant crises help us to ignore pain as does painkilling medication but that is simply over-riding the body's messages. Once you have taken notice and if the pain is persisting for a good reason, try a positive approach. Fear magnifies pain so be clear about your condition. Pain also brings rewards (in the form of sympathy and kindness) so be sure the pain is not persisting for this reason! If it is, get the attention you need in a more positive way. Try fun and laughter to help take your mind off it; seek love and affection, the magic behind 'kissing it better'.

The body also lets the brain know what it needs and messages are relayed back and forth to different body parts. We are actually born with our own appetite control centre which tells us when and how much to eat. Tests have been carried out with infants, and with World War II soldiers who, when left unattended but with a wide choice of foods, ate just the right variety and

---

THE DANGER SIGNS

1 Take notice of pain and forms of strain, such as headaches, skin rashes, indigestion, palpitations, insomnia and irritability. All of these are physical signs that your body is not coping well mentally or physically with some aspect. Try to locate the cause of tension.

2 Learn to recognise your own weak points and read them and make changes.

3 Know when to ask for outside or expert help. Some things require outside help before you can help yourself, e.g. unexplained bleeding, changes in your body such as lumps, moles etc., or mental symptoms such as confusion or depression. Don't suffer in silence; consult your doctor.

4 Pain is another defence mechanism – it is there for a reason so what is the cause?

The only problem with all these marvellous capabilities the body has is that in today's fast lifestyle, with new technologies and all kinds of new challenges, some of the body's basic signals are over-ridden or ignored. How many times do you resist the temptation to go to the toilet immediately and rush around holding on to a full bladder because you haven't got time to fit in this most basic of functions at the right moment? How many times do you ignore thirst and forget to drink so that the body is dehydrated before you even think about drinking?

The most commonly ignored homoeostatic response is the appetite control centre and this goes a long way towards explaining why so many people are overweight. Eating has become a fashion, a social experience and an overwhelming choice, all of which over-rides the basic message from the brain which is to eat only when hungry. Mothers tell children it is time for a meal so they must eat now; friends offer you afternoon snacks, and shops constantly tempt you with new products you should try. Listening to your body and its nutritional needs has almost become a thing of the past! Obesity, however, will only further limit the body's natural capacity to cope and puts further stresses and strains on the physical and mental frame.

Listening to your body and working with it should be one of the first approaches to relaxation and an easier lifestyle. Nutritional intake is an area in which we can all make improvements, whether we are overweight or not. Our diet is a factor that we can all control and one that benefits both the body and mind very quickly.

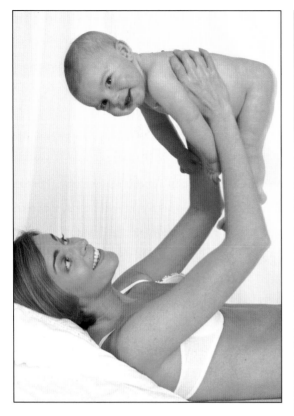

As infants, we are guided by the body's signals but as we grow older, we too often stop listening to these – often to our detriment, physically and mentally.

quantity to supply them with the energy and growth they needed.

Thirst is a very powerful way of telling us to replace lost fluids. This is particularly noticeable in breastfeeding mothers, many of whom report that the minute the baby starts to feed there is an instant desire to drink and thus replace what the baby is taking! Similarly in pregnancy many unusual cravings make nutritional sense when considered properly. For instance, one woman had a craving for ginger and liver! This sounds bizarre but ginger is a known nausea suppressor and liver is a good source of iron.

Your diet

What you eat really does have a great effect on how you feel and how you function as a personality. You have only to see the changes athletes and models make to their diets to realise that the way in which we fuel our bodies does have an effect on energy levels and fat levels. You should try to eat a varied diet – as they say, a little of what you fancy does you good! However, an over-reliance on any one or two things is not beneficial.

HOW HEALTHY IS YOUR DIET?

Answer the questions below to check if you really are eating as healthily as you might?

1. **Do you eat at least five portions of fresh fruit and vegetables per day?**
2. **Do you always look for low-fat options for milk, mayonnaise, sauces etc.?**
3. **Do you use olive oil or another pure oil for very shallow frying?**
4. **Do you avoid deep-fat fried meals?**
5. **Do you try to eat more fish and white meat rather than red meats?**
6. **Do you consume biscuits, cakes, pastries, cream pies once a week or less?**
7. **Do you choose whole-wheat pasta, bread and rice?**
8. **Do you eat pulses and beans regularly?**
9. **Do you use herbs rather than salt for flavouring your food?**
10. **Do you eat breakfast?**

    If you can change your eating habits so that you can answer "yes" to all the above questions then you will be eating a truly healthy diet, which is high in essential nutrients.

- Most people are aware these days that they should be eating plenty of fresh fruit and vegetables but how many of us actually do it?
- Most people are aware of lower fat alternatives to dairy products but do you actually buy them?
- Most people know that it is healthy to eat a high-fibre diet and that roughage is important but do you opt for whole-grain bread and cereals? Many of the bowel disorders becoming more common today are due to our intake of highly refined foods which don't provide the bowel muscles with anything solid to squeeze on! This means waste stays around longer and, along with weakening muscles, it can cause problems, such as toxic build-up.

DIET TIPS

Try to remember that there are no absolutely bad foods or miracle foods. It's just that some should be eaten only occasionally, e.g. chips, fish roe, fancy breads, full-cream milk, butter, ice cream etc., while others, e.g. wholemeal rice, pasta, bread, chicken and fish, can be eaten every day. Try to eat regularly but within the limits of when you are hungry. Take time to eat and savour your food, rather than eating on the hoof, which hampers the digestion and doesn't give you any rest.

Remember to drink plenty, too. You should drink at least eight to ten cups of fluid (ideally water) every day; if you don't, you may find yourself feeling tired and listless. Thirst is often

misinterpreted as hunger by people and thus not drinking adequately can add to a weight problem.

Try to keep tea, coffee, cocoa and cola to a minimum. All these drinks contain caffeine which is a stimulant. The irony is that many of these drinks are taken liberally at a time when a person is under pressure. The effect of these drinks is to temporarily boost the circulation while reducing feelings of tiredness. Yet if these drinks are consumed frequently (eight cups of coffee in a day plus a bar of chocolate, for instance), the side-effects can be very similar to the stressful symptoms that caused the increased intake in the first place! Caffeine is also addictive, and if it is consumed for any length of time and then withdrawn, people do suffer withdrawal symptoms and cravings.

All these things only serve to further increase pressure in your life when you are trying to alleviate it. If you can try to rely instead on relaxation and stress-management techniques, such as the ones in this book, then you can have the odd cup of coffee as a pleasure and savour its taste rather than gulping it down as a thirst quencher or pick-me-up.

CONTROLLING WHAT AND HOW MUCH YOU EAT

Controlling how much you eat is a twentieth-century occupation and spawns a billion pound dietary products industry. In terms of maintaining a desirable weight it is, however, a simple equation, as shown in the box below.

Dr Vernon Coleman refers to the appetite control centre which he says is "designed to ensure you eat just what your body needs, exactly when it needs it". However, once again, your lifestyle may be beyond your body's needs and so you may not rely on your stomach to tell you when to eat. Most people eat more out of social occasion, politeness and boredom than out of hunger. They eat more out of curiosity, tradition and timing than because their brains are telling them that they need nourishment. Because of this there is a tendency to miss the body's signals about what you should eat, and when tempted with all kinds of tasty

---

VISUALIZATION EXERCISE FOR APPETITE CONTROL

1 Picture yourself out with a friend at your favourite café or restaurant. You are about to order drinks and a meal or snack.

2 Try to remember the thoughts and feelings you have there. Try to remember those thoughts, after you have had one glass of wine, when you say: "Oh to hell with sensible eating. I want to enjoy myself!"

3 Now picture yourself saying "no" to the sumptuous cakes on display and opting for a salad. See yourself coping fine! You are still enjoying the bustling atmosphere, you are still listening to your friend's chat – you are still eating and drinking! Nothing has really changed; you have just made a wiser, more sensible choice over one small food item.

4 Practise this visualization exercise each time you are going out to eat somewhere where you might be tempted, and, if you can make it work, those little dietary changes will soon add up to large benefits, especially regarding your health and better weight control.

---

experiences, you may opt for the interesting rather than the nourishing.

We will not study weight control in detail here, but do try to make sensible choices when out having snacks. Choose foods that will sustain you – breads, pasta, vegetables which are complex carbohydrates and release energy into the system at a controlled rate – rather than going for the sugary option. Try the visualization exercise featured above as a way of resisting those high-calorie, low-nourishment snacks when you go out. They are only 'empty' calories.

THE ONLY DIETARY ADVICE YOU NEED

Food = Calories which are used for energy

Energy is used for activity

INPUT (calories) must equal OUTPUT (activity)

Excess input means calories stored for future use: FAT STORES INCREASE

Excess output means fat stores mobilized to produce enough energy: FAT STORES DECREASE

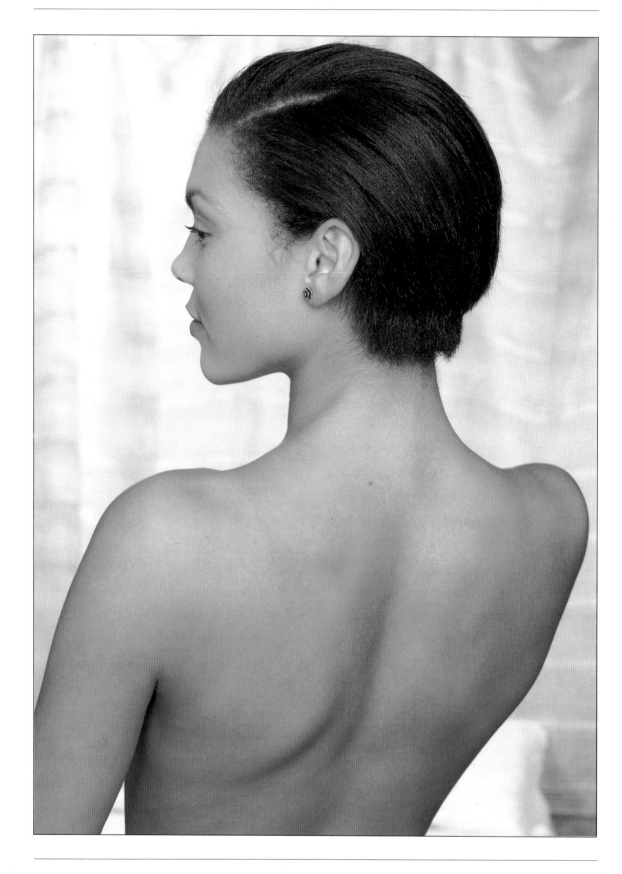

Bringing relaxation to everyday tasks

Stretches and direct exercises are not the only ways by which you can help yourself towards a more relaxed lifestyle. The way in which you carry out your daily tasks is an area you can improve and thereby adopt a new approach, both mentally and physically. In all the facets of your life, you can increase your awareness of where minor stresses occur. Sometimes you need to understand that less is more, and that tasks can be more effectively accomplished by simple movement and thought.

The mind and body are intimately connected, and thus any problems in your everyday life can be transformed into habit-forming physical tensions. If you can learn to release your physical tension, you can also help the mind to cope better. Thus you can think more calmly and move in a more efficient and beneficial way.

Unfortunately, relaxation is all too readily perceived as inaction: for example, as lying down and not moving. However, this is only one way of relaxing. There are ways of sitting, standing and walking that are economic and relaxed without being floppy or unsupported. There are ways of using the body's muscles, joints and pivots in the way they were intended so that muscle tone is perpetuated along with an easy poise.

Opposite: stand naturally and start to register the different tensions and imbalances in your posture. Use the Alexander technique to think your way through your body.

THE ALEXANDER TECHNIQUE

In the Alexander technique, students are encouraged to make full use of the body's natural alignment and balance. F.M. Alexander first noticed his own misuse of the body when faced with losing his voice as an actor. From this he evolved a way of using his body differently and alleviating muscular stresses. He then began to apply this formula to all types of people. The Alexander approach is more about eliminating stressful movement habits than adding new movements to the body's normal patterns. The body's natural balance is all too often ignored or over-ruled in pursuit of a busy lifestyle, and slowing down enough to recap on the body's natural resources can be very important. Rather than making changes to large body movements, try some of Alexander's commands which simply focus the mind on the area of tension without actually doing anything to it.

1 Start by standing and thinking your way through the body – don't tell your body to do anything different. Just note where there is tension and where there seems to be imbalance but don't readjust. Alexander stresses the value of first inhibiting habits rather than just overlaying with new ones. Therefore when you have noticed tensions in your body you can start to think about inhibiting the habitual reactions that normally occur.

2 Now, without making any changes, just think through some of these phrases: 'Neck release –

MONITOR YOUR BODY MOVEMENTS

Monitor yourself throughout the day and put as little physical effort into everything as possible. Slow down and pay attention to how you are doing things and you will find that incidences of clumsiness, accident and irritability decrease.

● Do you pick things up with one hand, hunching the shoulder as well?

● Do you carry bags all to one side, hunching one side of the torso and over-stretching the other?

● Do you use your whole body to twist the lid off a jar when you could just as effectively use the wrist action without using your shoulder?

● Try to use the body's natural strengths and flexibility. There are natural bending, pivoting and strength areas that provide for most physical tasks. Remember to bend and turn the body at its joints, as it was designed to do. When you lean over, bend at the hip joints rather than curving the spine. Twist above the waist where the rib cage can articulate, rather than transferring the twist lower down so that the knees become pulled in a way they were not meant to go.

● When standing, think about pulling up through the top of the head, dropping the chin. Keep the abdominal area lifted and try to think of the shoulders and pelvis as part of the back: as a well-balanced square from which the arms and legs can freely move.

● When sitting, don't allow the spine to curve and the stomach to slump, and try to resist the temptation to cross the legs, which not only puts uneven pressure on the bottom of the spine but also restricts circulation.

● When walking, try a little test on yourself. Face a mirror with a piece of blue tac on it, placed so that it is in the middle of your forehead as you stand. Now walk towards it, keeping the blue tac in the same place as you come nearer the mirror. You may become aware that you are swaying or favouring one side, as you walk. You might also notice similar mis-alignment from the way the soles of your shoes wear on one side or the other. These things do take time to correct themselves but the first step is increasing self-awareness which will help us to make small changes which can lead us towards greater ease of movement and an improved weight distribution.

head forwards and up'. Don't thrust your neck forwards or back in an effort to carry out this thought; simply let it rest in the mind, making minute physiological changes.

3 Now think: 'Back lengthen and widen' – in this way you are not shoving your body into severe postures. Then 'Back straight, stomach in'. You are suggesting to your body the concept of muscles lengthening and widening at the same time so that there is no greater pull on one area or another.

4 Now think: 'Shoulders releasing and widening'. If you go to bend the knees, think: 'Knees forward and away over the toes'. Remember that the main stable working areas of the body are the trunk and pelvis, both of which are strong and flexible. Above this the head should sit freely and without tension as these thoughts help the body to relax.

PERFORMING EVERYDAY TASKS

If you can start to notice where frustration and impatience make you approach tasks with more aggression than dexterity, then you can start to change your behaviour. Over the next few days, try to notice where you could approach tasks with a new relaxed attitude. Use your breath to pace yourself and draw back from frustrated fumbling! We've all experienced moments where the car key won't quite turn in the lock, or the hall cupboard door won't pull open. Instead of pushing at these things aggressively, forcing the offending object into submission, take a step back, calm yourself, drop your shoulders, inhale though the nose and exhale slowly. Now go back to the task and start again with as little physical effort as possible, and approach the problem logically! Even if the TV set does benefit from a good kick, if you do it with intention rather than frustration you will feel better at the end of the day!

Try another simple task and notice where there are other body parts involved which aren't strictly necessary; for example, how you hold the phone or a pen. Notice unnecessary tensions or undue force used. Notice any inappropriate shifting of weight or clenching of the

A 'fashionable slump' is not the best posture, although the shoulders are held low and relaxed.

buttocks, jaw or teeth. In this way you will start to become aware of even small pockets of tension or unnecessary muscle contractions that you can begin to release.

If you have an animal, for instance a cat, notice how it moves with grace and an economy of movement that involves tone and relaxed muscle; a minimum of superfluous movement. Think of words such as fluidity, lightness and balance as you move around. When you are standing still, think about the body being a series of building blocks, one stacked upon the other. If your posture is correct (see page 54) the frame should be well balanced with no stresses on either side and the head held comfortably on top. Somewhere between the military cliché of 'shoulders down, chest out' and the fashionable slump is the best standing posture. When you think about your shoulders don't tell yourself "Shoulders down" and thus force your shoulder blades down into the back, creating tension elsewhere. Instead, make yourself aware that perhaps you need to let go of the tension or hunching in the shoulder area. Making yourself aware of your tensions is the best way to get rid of them; ordering yourself to relax will mean nothing to your body.

CONSCIOUS TENSION TRANSFER

This is another useful way to relax certain areas. If you learn to site your tension in one area of the body rather than another, this can leave you not only free of stiffness in some areas but also actually help to strengthen the body in others. For instance, when entering a room full of people you might feel slightly tense; the most common reaction is to hunch the shoulders so the tension builds across the back of the shoulder blades and up through the neck. Try to become aware of this happening, and then consciously drop the shoulders and pull in on the stomach instead. Think about all the tension in your shoulders being transferred to strength in the stomach muscles. In modern dance techniques, the solar plexus and stomach are considered to be the root of movement and strength, and these areas are well equipped to put tension to good use.

Gripping the stomach will tone the muscles in this area and help keep the spine erect. It will also leave the upper torso free to relax and open up, giving the impression of a calm, approachable individual as opposed to a hunched, hunted one!

In the same way, when sitting, rather than cross-ing legs and arms in a protective, tense way, consciously transfer the tension into a straightened spine, allowing the limbs to be free and relaxed in an assured manner. This will encourage good blood flow to the legs and leave space for the stomach to be tucked in, maintaining balance and poise.

These changes take practice but even small instances will make a noticeable difference to the way you look and feel, if you practise them regularly so that they become automatic and unconscious.

A CLOSER LOOK

Certain tasks need a more exact approach if you are to succeed with them calmly and safely. Lifting heavy objects is an activity where people often incur unnecessary strains and injuries caused by lack of technique. You may be aware that you should lift with bent knees but are you really lifting in the correct way? Are you sure that even though your knees are bent you are not hingeing and taking all the weight through the back? Follow our guide opposite to check your technique.

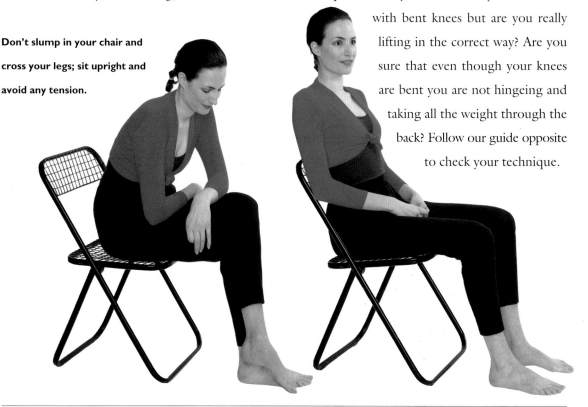

Don't slump in your chair and cross your legs; sit upright and avoid any tension.

BENDING AND LIFTING

Stand squarely facing the object with your feet hip width apart as close by to the object as is practical.

● Begin by bending the legs, taking the knees out over the line of the toes and taking the backside behind you. At this point there should be a straight line from the hips to the top of the head with the eyes focusing on the object to be lifted.

● The back should not be arched and the weight is over your heels so that all the work is being done by the large muscles in the legs and buttocks.

● Lifting up in the stomach for strength, lean forwards slightly and use the arm muscles to bring the object in close to your body.

● Keep the head in line with the spine, looking straight ahead of you.

● If possible, think of tightening the stomach muscles, and from this position press though the legs, squeezing the buttocks to straighten to standing.

Lifting in this way avoids the weight pulling on the back which is how so many injuries occur. This way the spine is stabilized and the bulk of the weight is lifted though the strong leg and buttock muscles, which are strengthened in the process.

CARRYING OBJECTS

In much the same way, carrying heavy objects should be the work of the arms and chest so as not to put pressure on the back.

Flex the stomach to provide a base to rest the object against rather than jutting out one hip which throws the spine out of balance and puts

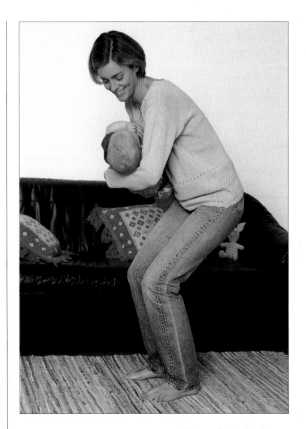

If you are lifting a baby or young child, pull him in close to you and bend your knees as you lift.

uneven pressure on the feet. When carrying a child, it is better, if at all possible, to link your hands between the child's legs and support the weight of his body on your arms, avoiding the weight pulling on just one side of the body. This also leaves your hands freer to hold something if necessary.

One of the best and most natural antidotes to stress is exercise. This is a life invigorating force, which, if practised regularly, can really make a difference to the energy with which you approach your whole life. Old and young people both need physical challenges in their lives, and exercise is one of the best ways to get them.

Exercise for health

Exercise is a great leveller and everybody can benefit from it, young or old, rich or poor. The body is a living evolving organism which needs the discipline of regular use. Muscles and the mind both need stimulation and regular challenges without which they become sluggish and eventually atrophy. Thomas Jefferson, one of the Founding Fathers of the United States, once said: "The sovereign invigorator of the body is exercise", and, practically speaking, relaxation and invigoration should be two sides of the same coin.

The body is powered by muscles contracting and extending; like the engines that move an aeroplane, they need constant maintenance and attention.

Muscles respond to work (or positive stress) and grow stronger and firmer to cope with the extra demands placed upon them. Nowhere is this truer than in the heart, which is the most important muscle of all, needing work to make it strong and efficient. With challenging exercise, the heart muscle develops and is then able to pump blood (with precious oxygen) around the body faster and with less effort. A strong heart muscle has more time to rest between beats and thus the body can exercise for longer without getting fatigued, as well as responding to physical challenges or emotional crises without raising the blood pressure.

By the same token, however, muscles need to be

TARGET HEART RATE

A more precise way to tell if you are working at the right intensity is to calculate your target heart rate. You should aim to work at an intensity at which your heart rate is pushed up to a range of between sixty and eighty five per cent, depending on how fit you are. An intensity of about seventy five per cent is probably the best level for fat burning. Do the following calculation to discover your limits.

Just deduct your age in years from 220 and then calculate 65 per cent of the figure you get for the lower end of the range. To work out the upper limit, deduct your age from 220 and then calculate 80 per cent of this. For example, if you are aged 32, do the following sum:

$$220 - 32 = 188$$
$$188 \times 65\% = 122$$
$$188 \times 80\% = 150$$

Therefore your THR is in the range of 122 - 150.

Now that you have your THR, use it to monitor your work-out. In the middle of your aerobic section stop briefly and take your pulse by resting your first two fingers over your artery (located on the outside, underside of your wrist below the thumb) for just 6 seconds and count the number of pulse beats. Multiply the figure by 10 and you should have a figure within your THR range.

If it is lower, then you are not working hard enough so you can put a bit more energy into your moves! If it is higher than your THR maximum, then slow down because you are overdoing it and will only feel stiff in the morning! Don't be tempted to go beyond your upper limit. If you are unfit, then take it gradually and slowly and try to keep your heart beat towards the lower limit of your THR.

brought back to their original relaxed state, and to do this a programme of stretching is helpful. Stretching expands the belly of the muscle back to its original length after it has contracted and thus allows the muscle more surface area to expel waste products and recuperate. Improved elasticity will also improve the tone of muscle. As this book aims to show you, efficiency in all aspects of life can be achieved without stress or exhaustion.

FINDING THE RIGHT SORT OF EXERCISE

The key then to gaining all these benefits from exercise is to find a form of activity that you enjoy and can do on a regular basis. Although many people join gyms or exercise classes, it is necessary to keep up attendance for a period of some months in order to really gain any lasting benefit. It will help, therefore, if you have a short programme you can do at home if you can't make it to your local class or sports session that will keep the activity level in your life constant.

Try to make this a programme you can fit into your life every other day and do it without fail! If you have a favourite routine you have learned from some sport or class you have attended, then use that – almost any exercise (as long as it is safe) will make a difference to the body if it is practised regularly. However, you should try to ensure that it has an aerobic component to it.

Aerobic exercise really just means exercise that uses all the major body parts for an extended period so that you breathe faster, requiring more oxygen and raising your heart rate, and the body

starts to metabolize fats for energy. Aerobic exercise reduces the physiological response to stress so that the adrenalin, sugar levels, heart rate and blood pressure are not raised so high. It also leads to a faster recovery from such reactions.

Even this small programme, if done regularly, will make a difference not only to your physical body but mentally too. An over-active mind and muscles that are jumpy and tight due to under-use, can make sleeping difficult. A short exercise routine before you go to bed will help calm the mind and tire the muscles ready for rest. Remember though that you have to teach yourself to do it regularly.

Home exercise routine

If you don't have your own personal exercise routine, you might like to try the following:

1 Start with a warm up that will get the blood flowing and the heart ready for action. March on the spot for several minutes. Move your arms back and forth in a jogging style. Start to lift your knees higher and move the arms in larger movements; up above your head or out to the sides of the body. Swing your arms from side to side for variation and make sure that you keep the marching fast and strong.

2 Now you should try to include your aerobic section. Try skipping, dancing, jogging on the spot – anything that gets you breathing harder but not so hard that you can't keep going for 15 minutes. If you can't keep the activity going for that long the chances are you're pushing yourself too hard. Slow down until you have built up your level of fitness. Check your target heart rate (THR) to see whether you are exercising at the right level (see the equation on page 42).

3 Next stand with feet hip width apart and perform some large bending movements. First bend your right leg with hands outstretched, so that you lunge to one side, and then bend the leg to the other side. Alternate sides slowly and then faster to increase your breathing.

③

(4)

4 Next bend both knees, taking the backside behind you into a squat position and press through the legs to straighten. Perform this move several times until you feel your legs begin to tire.

5 Finally, from a standing position, perform some star jumps on the spot – as many as you can do without getting too out of breath.

6 Now move on to some floor exercises. Sit on the floor and take both legs straight out in front of you. Whilst bringing your breathing back to normal, stretch your torso and arms over towards the legs. Remain in this position to feel a stretching out in the backs of the legs.

(6)

5

BENEFITS OF EXERCISE

● Many people believe that regular exercise can help you to live longer. Although this cannot be proved beyond all doubt, it is evident that exercise can improve quality of life as it enhances both the mind and body.

● Physically, exercise boosts the blood's circulation, helping to ward off heart disease and weakening bones (osteoporosis). It also encourages muscle tone which maintains posture, and keeps the body strong and flexible as well as guarding against excess fat.

● As exercise gives you time out to concentrate purely on yourself, it will give you increased physical energy, improve your self-esteem and generally reduce anxiety and depression.

7 Tighten your stomach. Lying on the floor with knees bent and feet flat, perform some small curl ups, lifting your head and shoulders up towards the ceiling. Lower and repeat for as many as you can (up to 50) Place your hands either on the thighs or behind the head to support the weight of the head.

8 Strengthen your back. Turn onto your stomach and rest your hands behind you on the small of your back. Gently arch the back to lift the head and chest off the floor. Repeat two or three times.

9 Finally come to a sitting position (in any position that is comfortable) and rest your hands by your sides. Take a slow breath into the body. Hold for a second and release. Repeat two or three times to bring you to a stillness that readies you for the rest of the day.

MOTIVATIONAL TIPS

- It can take twenty one days to form a habit so when you first start your programme promise yourself this amount of sessions before you skip even one session!

- Remember that once you have done even five minutes of exercise you will feel better so don't be tempted to skip your session because you are feeling tired.

- Unless you are really ill, even though you may feel you can't walk another step, a gentle exercise session will leave you with more energy than when you started!

- As you continue your sessions you will build more muscles and this will make you feel stronger and able to carry out even normal daily tasks without fatigue.

- Don't allow yourself the "I haven't got time" excuse. If you regularly exercise the heart, you will find running for the bus will not leave you exhausted for the whole morning, and with blood flowing more efficiently you will get through your tasks quicker, leaving you with more time.

- Don't set yourself impossible goals. If you think you can do a regular exercise session of thirty minutes, then make it fifteen minutes minimum. If you want to do more one day – fine. However, if you're feeling low on another day you should be able to do fifteen minutes. If you really haven't got time for even that, then make it five minutes that day but don't skip the session. As you continue to exercise you will notice such benefits that your body will start reminding you if you miss a session!

9

Relaxing the body

chapter three

ANOTHER WAY OF de-stressing the body is to think about being nice to yourself! If someone else told you to do this you would automatically think of doing all the things you enjoy! These might include taking some time off from your busy routine, doing some exercise and then having a relaxing sauna or a long hot bath, visiting your hairdresser or starting that novel you've been meaning to read for ages! All these instant desires reflect a more deeply held urge by our bodies and minds for a change of pace. The sympathetic nervous system goes into action during mental and physical activity while the parasympathetic nervous system (PNS) needs a period of peace and rest so that it can repair itself. Those repairs might be mental or physical, but the parasympathetic nervous system works only at times of relaxation, which only really means a change from what has gone before.

A change is as good as a rest!

If we lived lives in which there were long periods of inactivity or little mental stimulation, then relaxation might take a different form. However, in this age of constant bombardment from all kinds of media, relaxation is more about withdrawing for a moment from the modern world. The body and the mind crave opposites and contrasts – in other words, balance. Whether we give ourselves the balance we all crave is, course, another matter. Most people overwork, overeat and over-push themselves without taking time out to balance their lives. This is when life can get out of proportion and stress starts to build.

Both body and mind reflect their current states of health in each other. Emotional turmoils can be mirrored in knots and tensions in the soft tissues, e.g. muscles, while psychological attitudes can produce a defensive or stooping posture. Emotional and mental stress can show very clearly in physical terms, not just in muscle tone or posture but also in blood flow, which can be inhibited, and hormonal substances which can be out of kilter. Along with poorer lymph drainage, levels of calcium and lactic acid can increase, leading to pain, stiffness, cramp, tiredness and even hyperventilation.

When someone comes in to work with a headache or a feeling of nausea, the underlying cause may have more to do with their frame of mind than any physical factor. However, without the resources to sit everyone down and practise psychotherapy on them the easiest route is to prescribe a pill that will relieve the symptoms and allow that person to continue functioning for another day. So it is the individual's own responsibility to try and analyse his own bodily symptoms and provide balance in his own life. Yet how we treat our bodies and our minds is closely linked to our self-esteem. How much we care about ourselves is shown by how much we care for ourselves. Body neglect often shows mental neglect and vice versa.

Be good to yourself mentally and try to think positively. You can carry this on to a physical level by looking after your body and always listening to its reactions.

Posture

Poor posture can lead to impulses via the nervous system which create nervous activity and prevent mental relaxation. Yet over-stimulation and lack of balance can cause stressful symptoms, such as exhaustion or depression, leading to a lowering of self-esteem, and ultimately these feelings become mirrored in the body by even poorer posture! It is a vicious circle that will only be cured by taking time out to change things.

Start by standing in front of a mirror and having a good look at your body – see what it can tell you about your mental state and what it craves. There are some commonly accepted associations between bodily stance and mental feelings. Not all of these may apply to you but noticing your posture may give you some ideas!

Observing your posture

1 Stand facing a full-length mirror and look at yourself. Do not try to hold yourself in any particular way. Just stand as you would normally and observe your reflection.

2 Look at your head and neck. Does your neck seem strained or stiff? Does your head seem comfortably placed on your neck and shoulders or is it jutting out or held rigidly?

● Any odd positions here could be an indication of tension, either mental or physical.

3 Look at your face. Can you see care-worn lines? Does the face look older or younger than the rest of the body? Is the jaw tightly clenched or are the mouth and lips tightly pulled together?

● Severely defined lines in the face could be an indication of habitual tensions which become etched into our bodies. Some body therapists and health workers believe that if areas of the body are ignored or not fully nourished, they can be underdeveloped or appear immature. Is there a

Standing relaxed and straight gives a much better impression to the rest of the world than slumping. You will look more confident and self-assured, and your body will feel more balanced and comfortable. For advice on correcting your posture, see the practical advice in the panel on page 54.

blockage here and is there a reason for it?

4 Now concentrate on the shoulders. Is one raised up higher than the other? Are both your shoulders raised towards your ears or are they sloping forwards?

● Stooping, bowed or raised shoulders can indicate a poor self-esteem or too much going on mentally, which can lead to tension across the shoulder blades and neck.

5 Look at your arms. Ask yourself: are they held woodenly or rigidly by your sides? Are they relaxed at the elbow?

● Rigid arms indicate tension. Perhaps this could even be a fear of self expression?

6 Look at the solar plexus region. Is the stomach area weak and flaccid?

● Is this a neglected area? Do you move and react whilst ignoring this central area? Do you ignore your 'gut' feelings?

7 Next look at your torso. Is it slumping or even slightly bowed?

● This can also indicate poor self-esteem, or lack of physical use!

8 Look at the legs. Are they thick and unathletic? Are they sluggish?

● Legs can be seen as anchoring us to the real world; they represent foundation and support. Do you use yours enough for strong and vital

---

CORRECTING YOUR POSTURE

1 Make sure your body is well aligned and that your posture is comfortable. Most people tend to collapse in the lower back, have tense shoulders and rigid knees so that all the bend is in the spine.

2 Start by standing with your back against a wall. Have your heels far enough away so that your backside and shoulders just touch it. Now press your lower back towards the wall so that you feel your bottom start to tuck under just slightly and your stomach muscles pull in to help straighten out the spine.

3 Think only of dropping any tension there might be in the shoulders. Tilt the head down slightly to lengthen the neck and imagine a string pulling the top of your head towards the ceiling as your feet remain firmly on the ground. Your spine should feel as if it is lengthening.

4 Relax your jaw.

5 Your knees should be slightly bent and the hip bones wide. All limbs are relaxed rather than rigid. Now take a step away from the wall and then take a few more steps. Relax a little but try to maintain some of this good posture as you move around.

It may take you a while to let this exaggerated posture become more comfortable and natural but the basic premise is a good one. Try to be aware of your posture at all times, especially when tired or fed up. When you are standing, try to stand with the weight distributed equally on both feet. Avoid putting all the pressure on one foot as you jut out the hip and let the stomach muscles go! Keep your spine lengthening by imagining your coccyx (bottom of the spine) pressing down towards the floor and your head pressing towards the sky. Keep the stomach area strong and supportive. When you are seated, try to sit equally on both buttocks and do not cross your legs as this puts pressure on the spine and restricts blood flow to the legs and feet.

POSTURE POINTERS

POSTURE POINTERS

The body needs to be supported in its proper stacking system: shoulders over rib cage balanced on pelvis and hips, to leave the legs free but connected. In this way, weight is distributed evenly with no extra pressures on vulnerable joints or discs. The work and therefore the tone is gained by the muscles. The stomach and back give adequate space and support to all the internal organs.

movement? Do you day-dream more than you act?

Once you have looked at your body in this way it may make you stop and consider what you are feeling and going through at this time. You may also begin to see how emotions can be reflected in the body and how the body, in turn, can throw feelings back again.

Now try looking at your body again and this time correct the posture so that the body is relaxed and well balanced as it can be physically. Attitudes and emotions give rise to musculature patterns and postures. These, in turn, can give us unnecessary tensions and pains.

One of the most common complaints and reasons for absence from work is backache. This may be caused or exacerbated by poor posture, particulary in people with sedentary lifestyles and occupations. If you sit at a desk all day, huddled over a computer screen, you must pay particular attention to your posture, especially when seated. Make sure that your chair has adequate support for your spine and that you sit up straight and don't slump down in it.

Gentle toners

TONERS FOR THE BACK

One of the most vulnerable areas of the body is the spine. As already mentioned, the spine is often misused; it may be bent at the wrong angle, asked to carry the whole burden of weight alone or kept inflexible too long before it is suddenly asked to move dynamically. As human beings we have problems with our spines because we walk on two feet with the spine less supported than other animals who walk on all-fours. The fact that our bodies are upright much of the time means that the muscles supporting the spine – the erector spinae – are, in fact, very strong. However, it is always a good idea to keep the muscles in tip-top condition for periods when the spine is under extra pressure. This might be in times of stress; if you are forced to remain immobile or in awkward positions; or during pregnancy and after childbirth when the muscles and ligaments around the pelvis and back are softened. Perform the following gentle exercises two or three times a week to keep the back strong and healthy.

Back toner 1

1 Lie face down on the floor with legs straight and feet together. Rest your arms alongside your body with hands curving in to rest on the lower back.

2 Lift your head and shoulders off the floor. Keep the head in line with the shoulders rather than arching it back too far, but try to lift it up as high as you can so that you can see, for example, half-way up the wall.

3 Lower the upper torso and repeat up to 15 times.

● Keep the stomach pulled in and the buttocks tight as you perform these gentle movements up and down. This toner will strengthen the muscles that lie along either side of the spinal column.

Back toner 2

1 Start this exercise on all-fours with your weight evenly distributed between hands and knees. Stretch your left leg away behind you at the same time as you extend the right arm out in front. Do not lift the leg or arm higher than parallel with the floor, but stretch your two limbs away from each other extending the whole length of the spine. To keep yourself balanced, keep the stomach tight and the buttock of the extended leg really lengthening the leg.

2 Return the two limbs to the floor and repeat with the opposite two limbs. Repeat up to 15 times alternating legs and arms. This exercise will also strengthen the back and buttock muscles.

TONERS FOR THE STOMACH

There are numerous references in this book to 'pulling in' the stomach or to 'lifting it up' or 'keeping it tight' or 'strong'. This means the whole abdominal area, and it is one of the most important areas in the body. Being central, it is considered very much a part of the emotional body and it can be very, very strong. The abdominal muscles are important not only in providing protection for important internal organs, such as the stomach, intestines and reproductive organs, but also to help protect the lumbar spine, maintain the pelvic tilt and produce controlled movement of the trunk.

Whenever phrases like 'lift up' are used, this means that you should become aware of your muscles and harness their strength ready for action. But first you must make them strong! Here are some toning exercises to do just that.

● These two exercises combined will give you an all-round strong corset of muscle that will stabilize the back and give good movement and strength to the torso.

Stomach toner 1

1 Lie on your back, knees bent, feet flat on the floor. Extend both arms above your head and tilt your pelvis so that the lower back goes towards the floor.
2 Keeping your extended arms level with your ears, slowly and gently lift the head and shoulders off the floor. Keep the movement smooth but lift as high as you can and then lower. Your arms may come to rest where they are almost vertical but no higher. Perform only 8 repetitions and then rest before trying 8 more. Try to do these at least 4 times weekly.

Stomach toner 2

Lie on your back with knees bent but both knees resting over to one side. Rest both hands on one thigh and lift your head and shoulders off the floor curling over the top thigh. The body is twisted as you raise and lower the head and the hands reach as far over the thigh as you can. Lower and repeat the exercise up to 10 times on each side. The twisted starting position means that the oblique abdominals, the ones that wrap around the sides of the torso, are also being exercised.

For aches and pains

When you examined your body posture you may have found areas of tension. There are many ways, a lot of them described in this book, of dispelling tension, but you may find that with habit and time some areas have become more than just tense. Indeed, they are regularly stiff or aching. The lower back is always a prime area for aches and pains as are the shoulders or hips. Try these exercises for your problem spots!

PROBLEM WORK-OUT

Lower back exercise 1

1   Lie on your back, knees bent, feet on the floor, arms outstretched to both sides. Now gently bring the knees all the way to one side and rest them on the floor.

2   Take the head to look over the other side. If you are very stiff in this area

you may find this quite a pull so take it gently. Rest there for only a few seconds if this is at all uncomfortable. Now gently swing the knees over to the other side and the head the other way. Rest there.

3   As this comes to feel more comfortable, extend one leg so that only one leg is bent and use the opposite hand to pull the knee in to the chest as you roll over to one side. In this way you can take the stretch that bit further while still having control. Repeat the other way.

●   Try to do this exercise every night, particularly if your back troubles you during the day.

Lower back exercise 2

Another important aspect of spine care is to keep it limber in all its natural directions. The spine will articulate backwards and forwards and to the side to varying degrees. As we reach adulthood, we may forget that we should limber both ways

and it is only when we throw our weight back quickly to look upwards that something goes! Lie on your stomach with your elbows placed underneath you. Slowly straighten your arms and lift the head. Take the weight on your arms but push up until you feel the spine gently being flexed. Lower again and rest. Repeat 3 times, flexing slightly more each time.

Lower back exercise 3

Now lie on your side with legs straight, and curve up off the floor sideways. Use your side muscles as well as supporting yourself with your arms.

SHOULDERS

Shoulder exercise 1

1 Sit in a comfortable upright position with your back supported. Keeping your back upright with your pelvis tucked underneath you and stomach lifted, drop your head forwards. Remain in this position while you let the weight of the head pull out the tension in the neck and across the shoulders.

2 To increase this stretch further, take both hands and, linking them, rest them on top of your bowed head so that there is extra weight pressing down. As long as you feel a deep stretch, but no pain, let the full weight of the arms and elbows pull the head further forwards so that all tightness starts to release. Finally remove the hands and slowly raise the head.

Shoulder exercise 2

1 Slowly move your head to one side; press the ear towards the shoulder (without taking the shoulder up to meet it).

2 Rest there for one moment and then raise your arm (the same side as your head is resting) and place the hand on top of the head. You will feel the

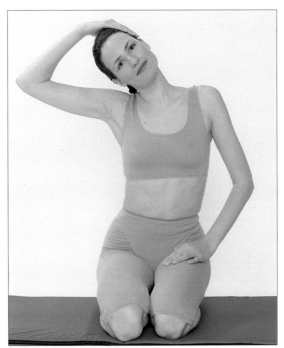

pull from the extra weight of your arm gently stretching the sides of the neck. Repeat this to the other side so that the muscles in the back and sides of the neck are stretched. If done regularly, this will help to keep this area more supple and free from knotting and tension. It can also help to prevent trapped nerves and cricked necks.

HIPS

Hip exercise

1 Sit with the soles of your feet touching, with the heels about 30cm/12 inches from your pelvis.

2 Hold on to your ankles without curving the back and pull the chest and head towards the ground. Feel the pull around the hip joints and stay forward only as long as is comfortable. Release to normal sitting. If this exercise is repeated regularly you will find that gradually you will become more flexible and be able to bring the feet in nearer

towards the pelvis and still press your upper torso forwards. The hip joints will have become just a little more relaxed.

OTHER TONING EXERCISES

You can also try other toning exercises such as head rolls, although these are not advisable in all cases. Consult your doctor if you are in any doubt. All the rolls described below will help keep these areas mobile and less prone to tension.

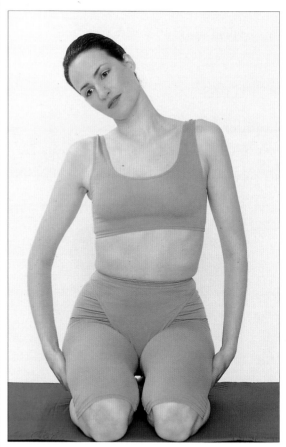

Head rolls

Drop your head forwards, so that the full weight of it hangs onto the chest, and then circle it round to

the right side, nose leading. Look over the shoulder and then tip the head to look up to the ceiling and then back down behind the other shoulder and, finally, to the front again.

Shoulder rolls

Pull your shoulders up to the ear lobes and then press them back and down, and then forwards to complete a circular limbering motion.

Hip rolls

Circle the pelvis in a large circle keeping the rib cage still, first one way and then the other.

Stretching

This is one of the best ways of relaxing muscles because it returns them to their natural state before they were contracted and shortened. Lengthened muscles are more limber, and if they are stretched regularly, muscles are less likely to cramp under stress or tear with a sudden movement. Try these stretches for other areas so that your body is ready for anything!

ALL-OVER STRETCH ROUTINE

1 Neck stretch

See problem work-out: shoulders 1 (page 59).

2 Shoulder stretch

Reach both hands above your head and link the hands. Press the hands and arms back behind the ears as far as you can. Hold and repeat 5 times. Next, reach both arms out to the sides of your body and press them out behind you as far as you can. Repeat 5 times.

● Both these exercises will keep the shoulder sockets flexible while stretching out the chest.

3 Side stretch

Stand with one hand on the hip and reach the other arm up to the ceiling and then slowly over to one side. Make sure you bend from the hip so that the spine is laterally flexed. The hand on the hip is there to support you so that the contracted side is not just crumpled but it is lifted and supported.

Feel your arm reaching upwards to keep the curved side well supported, not crumpled. Reach the extended arm out even further as you return to the upright posture. Repeat to the other side.

● As you get more proficient at this side stretch exercise, you can reach up with both hands and bend to the side. This will make the stretch more extreme and will also tone the sides of the torso as you come up to the starting position.

4 Quadriceps stretch

Because most of the movements we make are forwards and backwards on the same plane, some of the most used muscles in the body are the quadriceps. These are four muscles running down the front of the thigh which are responsible for lifting and extending the legs. Stretching these muscles regularly will keep your legs free of cramps and stop bulky muscular fibres building up.

Hold on to a wall for balance and bend one knee. Take hold of the foot and pull the heel gently towards the backside. As you do this, keep both knees together and press the hips forwards slightly as you lift the stomach. You should feel a stretch down the front of the thigh. Stop if you feel any pain in the knee joint. Repeat with the other leg.

5 Back arch

See problem work-out: lower back 2 (page 58).

6 Inner thigh stretch

Sit on the floor with both legs extended out to the side, with as big a gap as possible between the legs. Extend the arms and place your hands on the floor in between the legs. Now push the hands as far forwards as they will go.

When you can't reach any further, let your head hang forwards and relax the whole of the body towards the floor. The weight of the head will pull your upper torso towards the floor and you will feel a stretch in the inner thighs and possibly at the back of the legs too. Remain there for up to 20 seconds and then use the hands and arms to push you back to upright sitting. This exercise should be performed as regularly as possibe, i.e. 3-4 times weekly.

7 Achilles stretch

Finally, while still sitting, but with your legs together, reach forwards and take hold of your toes. If you have to bend your knees to do this that is fine. Then flex your feet, pulling them towards you. This will stretch the Achilles tendon at the back of the ankle. Then lean your chest as far forwards as you can towards your knees. Breathe out and hold momentarily. Slowly let go of the toes.

If you can perform some or all of these stretches regularly (3-4 times weekly), you will notice a marked increase in flexibility in most movements and a greater ease in achieving everyday tasks.

Breathing

This is the other main factor that affects your posture and the body as a whole. The most important thing about breathing is that it is a very physical thing. In fact, it is perhaps the most physical and basic function the body can perform and yet it is also an important tool for the mind. Not only is it the most basic requirement to keep the body alive and working but it is also the clearest pathway to inner thoughts and thus the recesses of the mind.

Breathing operates on a conscious and unconscious level; we can take notice of its flow or we can ignore it. Breathing always continues but changes all the time and responds not only to bodily demands but also to thoughts and emotional undulations, too. In the Western world it is often regarded as very much a biological function.

Inhaling air contracts and lowers the diaphragm, so that there is space in the chest cavity for the expanding lungs filling with air. The diaphragm is a dome-shaped muscle which divides the abdominal from the thoracic cavity. As the diaphragm relaxes, breathing out is achieved by expulsion of used air from the lungs aided by the rib muscles.

This is all very well but these breaths are also the most direct pathway to energies and emotions which exist on many levels of the conscious and unconscious mind. Because breath is so intrinsic to all bodily functioning, it is an expression and a reflection of our whole being. Many people believe that breath holds the power of growth and life, both spiritually and physically. Because it is a channel to and for all kinds of energies there is also great healing potential in breath.

HEALING

Breath (along with sugars) nourishes the brain (our major control centre). It changes as it reflects emotions, feelings, physical ailments and physical stresses. Therefore breath almost becomes a monitor for the way we feel and react, giving us indications to change our behaviour.

Our breathing is affected by changes in temperature; consider the changes that occur when you are very hot or freezing cold. Our breathing is also affected by tension; it is generally deeper when we are relaxed, involving movement of the whole rib cage. It is much shallower when aroused, with only the upper chest being used. If there is very great tension or distress, then hyperventilation can occur. Anxiety causes a bodily function to ready for action, and studies have shown that this can lead us to over-inhale and, in some cases, result in fainting. People who have been tortured develop hyperventilation as a protective capacity because it inhibits pain transmission to the brain and can lead to unconsciousness.

Learning to register and observe our breathing can help us physically: constant restriction of the diaphragm muscles can cause injury, bad posture and emotional stress. Slowing down frantic breathing can help our emotional state of mind.

LEARNING POTENTIAL

There is great learning potential in breath. Conscious breathing can actually start to take us on a journey inwards; it can expand our awareness of what is available to us in our bodies. Too often in the western modern world, the powers of the mind are ignored. We limit our focus on what is a physical reality and ignore everything that cannot be explained in terms of physical science. Yet we all possess the ability to turn our gaze inwards and search in that direction. We can all become aware of the instant pathway to an intimate look at our own experiences. It can lead to transcendental experiences, to the release of new energies and to spiritual guidance. Try the very simple exercise outlined here.

Breathing exercise 1

1 Just sit in whichever position you feel comfortable; it doesn't matter whether it's cross-legged or not, but try to keep your spine and neck lengthened. Now just become conscious of your breath flow. Don't try to alter it or regulate it in any way at all. Just notice it.

2 Notice where breath really seems to fill the body and where it is less evident. Notice if and where the breath seems to get stuck or stilted.

3 Notice how your breath flow responds to thought. Only notice – do not change anything!

Consciously registering our breath flow can give us an

inkling into our social, emotional and even spiritual selves. We can come to understand that logical, linear cause and effect thinking is not always the only way. Try another simple exercise.

Breathing exercise 2

Sit with eyes closed and notice your breathing. Register the in breath and the out breath. Don't change anything but start to picture. Picture colours: specific colours that you are breathing in and different colours that you are breathing out. Try breathing in red and breathing out purple. Breathe in blue and breathe out pink. Notice any emotional feelings that breathing those colours gives you. Only notice, that's all.

● The colours you choose are unimportant; it is just a first step to allying breath with conscious thought and emotions.

Yogic breathing

There are many other breathing exercises that can be done in all kinds of ways. Some are purely to illustrate the potential of breath whereas others form a basis for meditation or meditative practices such as yoga. One of the basic yogic breathing exercises is called the Pranayama. The active elements of the Pranayama include: inhalation, exhalation, breath retention, bhandas (which are ways of tightening muscles to control the breath), hand positions (for regulating breath through the nose) and four basic sitting positions. It also includes awareness of nadis and chakras, which are energy channels running along the body and intersecting the spine. Yogic breathing, then, is more about breath control. Try some basic nostril breathing as an introduction to breath control.

Nadi Sodhan: alternate breathing

1   Sit in any comfortable position with your eyes closed. Try to keep your spine as straight as is comfortable. With the first two fingers of your right hand tucked into the palm, use the right thumb to close over the right nostril. Breathe in slowly through the left nostril. The breath can be deep and can go into the chest, head and back, but there should be no strain.

2   When you want to exhale, release the blocking of the right nostril and block the left nostril (with the third finger of the left hand). The exhaled breath flows out of the right side. Now breathe in through the same nostril and change fingers to breathe out through the other side.

● Always breathe in through the same side as you have exhaled and change nostrils at the beginning of each in breath. If you find this at all difficult, concentrate on the exhalation. This is the part that means releasing and letting go of breath. All kinds of things can occur with this breathing; if you feel dizzy or start to pant or feel short of breath then stop the exercise and return to it later. However, you might feel relaxed and more centred as your two brain hemispheres are united and you enter a natural harmony.

Directed breathing

Once you have tried this more controlled breathing you can also try directed breathing, which relates directly back to the body.

1   Sit once again and start to observe your breath flow. Notice where it flows easily and where it seems to have trouble reaching. Ask yourself some questions about this. Are these particularly tense areas? Are they areas of your body you don't like or are not in touch with much? Are there pressure filled pockets of emotion which are blocking the breath pathway?

2   Now try one of two things: first, consciously start to direct your breath into those tension filled areas. Be insistent, breathe in and push that breath up into those areas. Feel and believe in the breath flooding the tension and emotion and diluting it into release with each inhalation.

3   Now, secondly, concentrate on the exhale and in this way you flush out all those pockets of resistance: resistance to the clear flow of breath through and around the body. Breathe in and, as you breathe out, try to release any tensions and any emotional worries, and thereby cleanse both your body and mind.

SUMMARY

You will notice how breath can really affect us, both mentally and physically, if we just become aware of it – how we can use breathing to our advantage in relaxation of mind, body and spirit. This is why it is at the basis of many meditation programmes and plays an important part in dance, sport and psychotherapy. After practising these exercises you will see how intricately the mind and body are intertwined and how what we do with one 'half' affects the other.

Practical relaxation exercises

Now use the mind to order the body and see how this affects your relaxation levels.

Work and unwork

Start by lying on the floor in a comfortable position, eyes closed. You are going to start working through your body giving orders to different body parts, then relinquishing those orders and next noticing the different feelings that arise as an aid to relaxation.

1   Start with the shoulders. Tell yourself to press your shoulders down towards your feet. Actually make this movement and hold it there, just for a second, and then tell yourself: release.

2   Once you have released, just 'watch' with your mind's eye and feel the area you have just released. Notice the changes. Notice how it is freed from the constriction you placed on it and how it can open out and let go of any tension. In this way, you will be moving different areas of your body towards actual physical, muscular relaxation.

3   Follow this whole sequence through. To start with it might help if someone else can read the instructions out to you so you don't have to keep looking at the book! But after a while you will remember them yourself and will be able to talk yourself through them. In the box opposite are your self orders.

Go back through the sequence, just noticing all the parts of your body that are now released. Travel in different directions to all these points and you will come to realise a great ease in your body.

THE 'FARMER AND BLOW'

Some relaxation methods work by tensing and then relaxing muscles in different body parts. Although this can help to get really in touch with the muscle and locate exactly where the feeling should be, it also means that each part of the body is systematically tightened which can lead to an accumulation of tension even as you are trying to ease it! Try this method instead which first centres all the tension in the fist and then allows all the tension to drain out through the fist.

1 Start by lying down with eyes closed in as comfortable a position as you can find. Now start-ing from the shoulders, begin to visualize all the tension that exists in the shoulders. 'Look around' that muscular area and notice all the pressure and aches or pains.

2 Once you have a good 'picture' of any problems and unease, then clench your fist on your dominant side. Now relax the fist and, as you do so, picture the tension in the shoulder area releasing and flowing out through the relaxed fist. This hand is the route by which all tension travels from whatever part of the body out into infinity and away!

● Use this sequence to zoom into all or just

SELF ORDERS FOR RELAXATION SEQUENCE

1 **Shoulders:** press your shoulders down towards your feet. Release them. Notice the new length between the ears and the tops of your shoulders. Notice how the muscles across the shoulders have ceased being pulled and can lengthen and widen as they relax.

2 **Rib cage:** press the ribs forwards, pulling the back of the ribs together. Release. Notice the spine sinking towards the floor and the ribs falling in to their natural position. The rib cage is widening and filling with breath. Take a deep breath. Hold. Release.

3 **Arms and hands:** straighten your arms and flex back your hands. Release them. Notice the arms falling back on to the floor to be supported. There is no need for any muscles to be holding the arms in a certain position. Let them lie in whatever position they fall. Now notice your hands: the fingertips or backs of hands are fully resting. Appreciate how rested your hands are – as if someone is holding them. Let this image travel back through your arms all the way to the shoulders. When you reach the shoulders think of the head.

4 **Head:** press your head back into the floor. Release. Notice that the head is supported and without strain. Picture your head being pulled gently away from your feet. Notice the elongation of the spine.

5 **Buttocks:** squeeze your backside tightly, pushing the hips slightly towards the ceiling. Release. Notice the muscles letting go and the weight of your body falling into the floor, flattening the muscles and squashing any tensions away.

6 **Legs:** bend the knees and draw the feet in towards you. Release. Notice a more comfortable leg position with no tension in the knees.

7 **Feet:** flex your feet, toes towards shins. Release. Notice how the calf muscles are untightened. The feet and toes are passive. Notice the untightened state of the legs, buttocks, rib cage and waist. Take a deep breath. Hold. Release.

SPINE RELAXER

This relaxation exercise works on the principle that 'there are other ways of being' (John Gray Alexander Technique). The body always finds the easiest way of being and moving. Therefore if we impose certain conditions on the body it will make adjustments. Use two juggling balls, which are round and slightly soft, for this exercise.

1   Place one underneath and in the middle of the shoulder blade and lie flat for a few minutes on top of it. There is no movement or adjustment to be consciously made, only what the body sees fit to do itself.

2   Continue lying in this position and start to notice where the back touches the floor and where it is lifted. Notice the distribution of weight, which limbs are fully touching and others only partially resting. You should not feel uncomfortable with the ball pressing into the shoulder blade; in fact, you should feel tensions starting to release from all around this area. If the pressure of the ball is at all uncomfortable, then re-position it more cen-

trally and give yourself a few seconds to see if this will make a difference.

3   Now take the second ball and position it in the middle of your buttock (the opposite one to the shoulder blade). Rest in this position and observe the changes. The two balls will start to lengthen the spine slightly, drawing it out as it copes with the raised positions. Picture your spine lengthening and releasing tensions held between the discs as it stretches.

4   Change the balls to the opposite sides and repeat the process. Notice where the back of the body touches the floor and where it is raised. Notice where the muscles flatten and relax to accommodate the protrusion.

5   Finally, remove both balls and spend the next few minutes watching your body readjust to its new resting position. Picture the spine coming to rest on the floor longer and with less tension. Take several long, deep breaths, very slow on the exhale, and open your eyes.

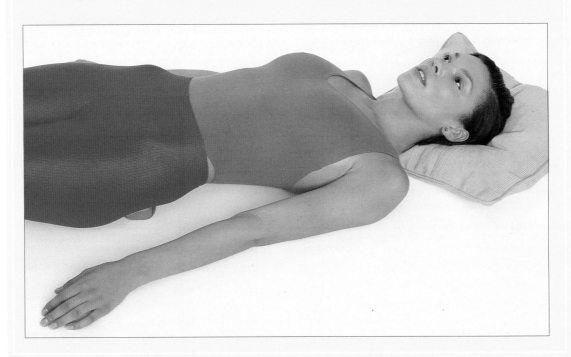

some tension areas in your body, and use the clenching fist as a pathway to relieving tension. Work from your shoulders systematically down the body towards the feet. Then come back up the body and focus on the head and then the face. Picture any tension in the lips, eyelids, mouth and jaw, and use the fist to relax the face as well!

SLEEP

One of the most important and effective relaxers of all is sleep. It refreshes the mind and body, allowing your subconscious to come to the fore. The body has, and is, affected by many cycles: the cycles of motion and activity and then winding down to rest, and sleep is the most essential one. When a person becomes stressed or unable to relax and their sleep becomes disturbed, then the situation can become very serious.

Sleep should be as natural as your unconscious breathing, yet with pressures of work and socializing, it can start to elude us. There are natural rhythms to sleep and various stages that are important, but due to false sleeping patterns and drugs, i.e. sleeping tablets, these can often be disrupted.

The alpha stage is the first state, which is somewhere between being truly asleep and awake. The dream state then follows, taking up to about twenty five per cent of sleep, which is when the maintenance of the mind takes place. After the dreaming stage, sleep becomes lighter, but this is where hormones from the pituitary gland are produced and this has the restorative and refreshing effect on the body that you can feel after waking from a good night's sleep. Many people can function on small amounts of broken sleep, e.g. nursing mothers or night workers, and it need not necessarily become a problem. However, a sudden problem with sleeping can indicate an imbalance in routine that just needs correcting.

Relaxation and other wind-down techniques, as detailed in this book, will help to keep you relaxed throughout the day so that sleep is a pleasant conclusion. Do try to avoid drinking stimulants such as tea, coffee and cocoa before settling down for the night, and you should also make sure that you have an adequate intake of B vitamins. The amino acid tryptophan has also been shown to have some beneficial effects on insomniacs and is a relaxant and sleep inducer without any known side-effects. Foods that are rich in tryptophan are: dairy products, fish, soya beans and nuts.

Mental awareness

chapter four

THE ART OF RELAXING is very much about getting the mind and body to work together in harmony and making them work for you! You can help your mind to relax your body by concentrating on physical sensations. Exercises, such as the bodily relaxations described already in Chapter 3, use the mind to focus inwards on sensations and tensions in the body. The mind can then work with this information and make choices, encouraging the body to let go of tensions or release contracted muscles, leading ultimately to a more relaxed physical state. Challenges are options that require a response or action of some kind, and it is how we react and deal with these that dictates whether the effect on us as individuals is positive or negative. If the challenges are too complicated, this can create an imbalance between demands and resources and lead to a feeling of pressure.

Self perception

The body can also play its part in relaxing the mind. Any physical pursuit can help to concentrate the mind so that it is distracted from everyday thoughts or mundane patterns of worry. A good hard game of tennis can make your mind focus on the competition of the game, while a relaxing jacuzzi bath can highlight the pleasure and sensations of the warm bubbling water over your skin, a diversion from mulling over nagging worries or decisions.

The mind, however, is a very flexible and powerful tool and you can use one part of it to influence another part! Rather like you can train your body to react in certain ways, e.g. dropping your shoulders when you feel tension rising or breathing slowly when you feel anxiety building, you can also use your mind to improve your mental health! If you can learn to think in a very positive way it will change the way you feel. Thus although you cannot change the traffic jam in which you are stuck or the irritating behaviour of a particular shop assistant, which are both stressful factors in your life, you can change the way you

HOW GOOD ARE YOU FEELING ABOUT THINGS TODAY?

Becoming aware of how we perceive situations and ourselves can be the first step in starting to think more positively. Try this quiz at various times over the next few months and see whether, with a little letting go and relaxation, your score improves. Answer the questions below, rating them on a scale of 1-5 where 1 is low and 5 is highest, and add up the total score to see what your level of self perception is.

1   How determined are you?   1 2 3 4 5
2   Rate your level of assertiveness.   1 2 3 4 5
3   Are you happy with your general routine?   1 2 3 4 5
4   Rate your level of understanding and patience with others.   1 2 3 4 5
5   How happy are you with your figure?   1 2 3 4 5
6   Rate your level of commitment to projects.   1 2 3 4 5
7   Are you happy with your concentration levels?   1 2 3 4 5
8   Rate your quickness of mind?   1 2 3 4 5
9   Are you happy with the way you treat your partner?   1 2 3 4 5
10   How high is your energy level?   1 2 3 4 5
11   Are you happy with the division of work, rest, play etc. in your life?   1 2 3 4 5
12   Rate the level of relaxation in your life.   1 2 3 4 5
13   How friendly does the world seem to you now?   1 2 3 4 5
14   How likeable do you see yourself now?   1 2 3 4 5

react to these situations. In the same way, although you cannot change the world by thinking about it you can change the way in which you perceive it!

SCORES FOR TESTING YOUR LEVEL OF PERCEPTION

15-30: Your view of yourself and your life is rather dull at the moment. You are obviously feeling rather low in energy and spirit. Try to find ideas and activities that enthuse and inspire you. See if you can practise some of them to help you lift your spirits a little. There are lots of techniques in this book that you can try.

30-45: Use some of the relaxation methods outlined in this book to help you unwind more at the end of each day so that you can introduce more tranquillity and time for reflection into your life.

45-60: You seem to be in fairly good spirits. Look at where you had lower scores to identify the areas in your life that may need some improvement. Use some of the relevant sections in this book to give you ideas for achieving this.

60-70: You are feeling satisfied with life at the moment. If you can feel this way most of the time, it would be great! Use this book to help you stay feeling this way and to help you maintain a sense of balance in your life.

Note: Answering these questions can make you more aware of some of your feelings and the way in which certain attitudes you hold may influence how you feel about things. They may even have become habits which are colouring the way you think. For instance, we all have problems, some small, some larger which will take more time to solve, but we also have good things in our lives which make us happy, and things that we hope for and so on. If you focus on all the problems in your life, forever mulling over how to solve them or how many different ones you have, your world will be full of problems! Alternatively, if you focus on the good things in your life, you will feel much happier! It sounds so simple put like this yet many people forget that they can change their attitudes and thereby change the way they feel.

Look again at your answers to the quiz and your overall rating. Is there something you can do to boost your score? Is it a question of giving yourself more time for yourself, or of changing the way you approach certain issues? When you have tried some of the techniques for mental and physical relaxation which are featured in this book, go back and do this quiz again. You will find that your answers are significantly more positive!

Positive thinking

Some of the problems, not all, that you encounter and may permeate your life are as much a part of your mental process as they are of your actual physical life. Try to be positive in your thinking and then you will get the most out of any situation. Try the positive pointers outlined below.

● If you're feeling a bit fed up, focus on something that you have achieved recently. It doesn't matter whether it's a small thing. It doesn't matter that it may be smaller than the number of big issues

Always try to think positively and banish any negative thoughts. Remember something that you achieved today rather than dwelling on any problems.

you completed such a task in such a short time. Don't think that you might not finish your project. Instead, be positive and just think how in three months' time you'll wonder how you ever got so worried about it in the first place!

● Look at the beauty around you. Take time to notice that there are delightful and beautiful things in your world. Try to focus on these for a moment before returning to your everyday thoughts.

● Withdraw from a difficult situation and imagine that you are not in it but watching it. Try to visualize reading a novel about what is happening to you at the moment, and how funny or interesting it might be to an outsider.

● Try always to 'have a go' – on balance more people regret not having done things than doing them. So take a leap of faith and try it!

● Do not compare yourself with others – try to evaluate your life on your own principles and standards, not by those of other people. Meditation is a great aid here to looking inwards (see page 92).

● Smile at the world even if you don't feel that great. People respond more positively to happy, bright people and you might even end up changing your mood! If you're feeling low, then a chance conversation started on the bus can lift your spirits. Business people are more likely to remember you if you look happy and relaxed, and you will find that your own body and the rest of the world responds if you keep a cheery disposition!

that are worrying you. Focusing on an achievement will help you to keep things in proportion.

● Try to learn from difficult situations even as they are happening. An important part of positive thinking is taking a step back and not panicking. Stop, focus your mind for a moment and try to understand how the thing that is frustrating you could yield some positive aspects. It might be that you have a tight deadline hanging over you that makes you feel pressured every day. There may be many different tasks to accomplish for which you feel there is not enough time.

While these are real concerns, it is also helpful if you can picture yourself after the project is completed. You will have tackled all the difficulties and be left with a sense of deep achievement that

- Don't write off whole periods of your existence. Every time you say, "Oh, I'm having a bad day" you have written off a whole twenty four hours. It also means that every new situation is a further opportunity for you to confirm your already dreary outlook. Tell yourself: "Well, that didn't go too well but things could improve". Try to find something positive, however small, in each new day. Keep things in perspective and don't over-react.

- Assume the best – not the worst. Assuming the worst so as not to be disappointed is the wrong way of positively approaching your life! Always assume, or hope for, the very best.

FOCUSING THE MIND

It helps with positive thinking if you know how to focus and relax your mind. Most of the time you are using only part of your mental energies; your attention is subject to a thousand distractions and thus your thinking becomes cluttered and issues can seem more pressing than they really are.

If you can learn to relax your mind, like you relax the body, it can slow down and allow you to exist in the present moment more calmly. Try some of the following suggestions for slowing down your thoughts for a moment, and you will start to discover greater perspective in your life.

1 Stop thinking!

No-one can stop thinking; it is impossible. If you start trying not to think, you will only end up thinking about how to stop thinking! What you can do, however, is to withdraw from your thoughts and then become more of an objective spectator.

Picture your mind as a blank canvas or a dark sky over which fireworks of thought explode and whizz across. Do not try to eliminate or to hurry these thoughts; just slowly observe them as they pass by. Allow your thoughts to come and go while resisting the urge to follow each one; get involved in it and then act on it. In this way, your brain will slow down its mad 'babbling' and you will feel less pressured.

2 Counting

If you find it difficult to let go of your thoughts, then try counting slowly as you breathe. Watch your thoughts and try to resist following them, but if you can't achieve this, then try to turn your attention to the count as you breathe out.

3 Active attention

Passive attention means that thoughts, impressions and feelings are noticed and followed in a higgledy-piggledy fashion. However, active attention needs active exertion. As you work and think, try to keep your attention on the task in hand. Be strict with yourself and each time your mind wanders return it to the task. As you keep refocusing your attention, your 'mind stillness' will improve.

4 Still your body

One sign of fragmented attention is fragmented movement. For example, if you are in the theatre, it is easy to tell if whoever is seated in the row in front of you is fully attentive to watching the play. People who sniff and sigh, move their heads this way and that, and wriggle in their seats are having some difficulty concentrating. Rapt attention is usually accompanied by still body posture.

To still your own body, find a comfortable position and don't allow yourself to move. Now concentrate on what you are doing or watching; draw your attention away from physical distractions and focus your thoughts fully on your task. After a while you will notice that you fidget less and feel less physical discomfort. This is because you are now channelled into mental exertion.

5 Interest your mind

Challenge yourself to remain focused – nothing focuses the mind more than interest. Try to find interest in projects to help you concentrate. If you are at a party full of what you perceive to be not 'your kind of people', then make a positive effort to find someone and start a conversation. Ask that person about himself/herself. Ask the sort of questions you wouldn't normally think of asking. Be inquisitive and you might discover you have things in common or new interests in subjects that you wouldn't have thought about ordinarily.

6 Opening the mind

Don't close off avenues of your mind by saying "I don't agree with that, I won't discuss it", or "I have absolutely no interest in that". There may come a day when you will. Tom Winjee, author of *Mental Fitness*, says that "a fit mind is a full storehouse of personal interests". Rather like you need to work out the body in a variety of ways, so you need to exercise your mind. Just as strength, stamina and

Opposite: open your mind to new possibilities. You may discover something you've never even considered.

flexibility work must be incorporated into your physical routine, in the same way the mind needs new and absorbing challenges to give it a change from its everyday journeys. A new hobby can open up a whole new world of interest, and even learning a new word can suddenly make you hear it everywhere you go. Try walking to your local newsagent and notice something new on the way there, e.g. people's facial expressions. Notice something new again on the way home: perhaps a beautiful tree you never really paid attention to before or a building facade you hadn't noticed. When you are at the newsagents, buy a magazine on a subject you wouldn't normally look at. Read it, and open up your world to new possibilities!

Creative thinking

As well as thinking positively, creative thinking is a great aid to coping mentally and to mental relaxation. It is really just a way of letting your mind take other paths and thinking routes than it normally would do. Like the body, if the mind is used for the same old tasks without variation, then it becomes set in its ways and stiff. We often think about the same few topics in the same few ways without even realising it. In this way, the mind becomes bored and fatigued as it treads familiar roads without finding new thoughts or solutions. Many people say it is at the most unlikely times that

they get their flashes of inspiration; you might be lying in bed, reading a novel or even in the bath. However, it is at these times that the subconscious mind is given room to manoeuvre and can come up with new ideas! Creativity is not just about coming up with new and original thought. It might involve adopting old ideas but for a new purpose – or finding a new solution to an old puzzle.

WHAT DOES CREATIVITY MEAN TO YOU?

Put down this book for a few moments and go and do something creative. Do it now!

Well, what did you do? For instance, did you draw something? Did you choreograph a dance? Did you come up with an idea for making extra cash? The point is that creativity is different for each of us, and we can use what it means to us in very different ways.

CLEARING THE BODY READY FOR MENTAL ACTION

In order to free the mind, you might start with the body. It might be that you are feeling rather tense after a hard day. The brain can turn social problems into bodily tension and it may be a good idea to relax your 'outer shell' first.

Slowing down the body

Seat yourself in a comfortable position; now start to focus your mind on the body. Notice the different physical feelings and sensations in your body. Guide your mind to what your muscles, fibres and sinews are feeling. Picture what your body looks and feels like from the outside. Now picture what it feels and might look like deep inside. Keep pulling back your mind to this task.

Keeping alert

It may be that you are feeling rather too relaxed and sleepy when you want to do some thinking. In this instance, adopt a posture that is slightly uncomfortable or requires some physical effort. If you are in public you could try mimicking some of the postures of the people around you. Don't do anything that is too painful or is going to take your mind off what you are doing, but use it as a way of staying alert. Another way to refocus your attention, if you find it slipping, is to say to yourself: "Where am I now?" Make yourself stop and notice – really look at and listen to your surroundings. Take stock of where and with whom you are, and what that person is saying to you exactly. Thoroughly plant yourself in the here and now, and for a moment rid yourself of all other anxieties.

CLEARING THE MIND READY FOR ACTION

Anxieties, everyday thoughts and preoccupations are always clouding our minds. They keep our thought pathways busy with nagging doubts and reminders of tasks not yet done. If you are really trying to concentrate your mind (if you are trying to find a solution to a problem), it can still be distracted by other thoughts. You may start thinking about the presentation that is due next week, the trousers you bought that are the wrong size or even the pile of washing up in the kitchen! Try taking some time out before you address your mind to the real problem so that you can label all these nagging thoughts in your mind as having been 'dealt with'.

Take a blank sheet of paper and write down all the things you are worrying about. Write down everything that is on your mind and bothering you, however trivial or small. Set it down on the piece of paper in black and white. Picture these worries being drawn from your mind on to the paper. Now tear the paper in half and file it or throw it away. Your worries haven't disappeared but they have been acknowledged and taken into account. For the time being you are free to think of other things!

DECISION-MAKING

Life is full of many hundreds of decisions that have to be made every day: some small, like whether to take the bus or tube to work; some trivial, such as whether to wear black or brown shoes today; and some more portentous, such as whether to change jobs or move house. It is when you are faced with many decisions, large and small, that the mind becomes stressed, over-anxious and begins to repeat the same old patterns of thinking.

When making decisions, thinking creatively also means thinking clearly.

Before focusing on how and what to decide, consider how you normally make your decisions. For example, are they made from habit rather than conscious analysis?

TRY SOME SELF-ANALYSIS TO HELP YOU REACH YOUR DECISIONS

1 Make sure you know what you want! This is the best way towards making the best decision and is also the part of decision-making that is most overlooked. Make sure you know what you would like the final outcome to be, otherwise the means (as opposed to the end) can be thought about for ever.

2 Having decided on the 'end' you would like to achieve, make sure you know what the costs may be.

3 Now as a simple chart for decision-making, make a temporary decision one way or the other. Go with your gut feeling, and if you still can't decide, then flip a coin.

4 Stick with that decision and make a list of the pros and cons of that decision. Write down everything you can think of.

5 Make sure your pros and cons don't contradict each other.

6 Now go back to your 'pros' and give each one a mark out of 10. Mark it according to how important that 'pro' is. Do the same with your 'cons'.

7 Total up your two scores and see which one is the higher. This will give you your decision.

The deeper senses

There are many other devices and ways to make a decision but one of the best is that attributed to Isaac Newton. Apparently he would flip a coin labelling heads to one alternative and tails to the other. If when he flipped the coin and discovered he was happy with the outcome, he would go with it. If he found he was disappointed with it, he would change his mind to the other alternative, knowing

he had made the right decision! Think about it! This only goes to show that when we allow our deeper senses to help make our decisions for us we can come up with a decision we can live with and accept.

Sometimes we have to allow our subconscious feelings to come to the surface. Making a decision and then noting how we feel about it can help us to assess our degree of satisfaction with it. However, on other occasions when we need to take a decision, making time to relax afterwards can help our intuitive self to start to work. As your mother will tell you, 'sleeping on it' can allow the subconscious mind to surface.

Using our deeper senses can help in many ways. It can help us deal with upsets, disappointments and frustrations. It can also let us truly relax and enjoy the present. Being aware of our subconscious can give us a better understanding of ourselves – our hopes and desires, our motivations etc. This can demystify many depressing issues in our minds and help us to view the world and our behaviour differently. Thus relaxing your mind and body can encourage your deeper senses to be 'heard'.

Try to keep your mind open to new possibilities and new alternatives so that you don't narrow down your world. Modern psychotherapy uses the emotions and the mind's 'voice' as guides to inner

Opposite: decision-making is often a difficult process, especially if you don't sort out what you really want the outcome to be. Don't make decisions by default. Become more aware of your subconscious, relax your mind and try to understand your inner self.

turmoil and also to help increase awareness of the indications of our deeper feelings. Often our real desires lie buried or hidden deep within ourselves, and it can take professional help to peel back the layers and reveal our true feelings.

Staying in control

In order to feel relatively happy and balanced, most people need to feel in control of their lives. It is when multiple situations in your life become out of control and intolerable that you can start to get depressed or saddened. Most common depression is usually due to more than one single factor. Instead, it is a series of events that gradually pulls down a person into lethargy and despondency. If you can feel in control of your day-to-day life it will help even bad situations seem more manageable.

Many of the decisions we make in everyday life are not made by the process described in our decision-making section (see page 81) or indeed by any other formal decision-making process, but by default. Situations exist not because you choose them but because you have not made a conscious decision to change them!

For example, not exercising, not taking time out to relax, eating the same old foods and staying in a tired relationship are all decisions made by default. They need a new approach and a conscious decision to change, yet these default situations can have more of an impact on your life than anything else. Passively accepting decisions that were never quite your choice in the first place can cause you to

THE 'MUST HAVE' MANUSCRIPT

1   Start with a wish list. Make a list of all the things you would like to do, see, have, experience etc. Write down absolutely everything you can think of: large, small, obvious or even secret! Take a piece of paper and write it all down now!

2   Now divide these wishes into categories, e.g. material, career, relationship, recreational, personal growth and so on.

3   Now you can start to analyse these wishes. Look at your list and then ask yourself the following questions:

- Which are the most important?
- Are any of these wishes truly impractical and, if so, why do you still want them?
- Do any of your wishes conflict with each other?
- Are these all your own wishes or have they really come from somebody or something else?
- What would you be like/ be doing if you didn't have this wish?
- How much positive satisfaction have you gained from having this wish and how much more would you gain if it were fulfilled?
- When did you begin wishing for this?

Answering these questions will help you to delve deeper into what you really do desire. You may need to alter your list. Maybe you will realise that some of your wants are influenced by advertising or someone else's opinion. You may find that some of your wishes are very deep seated and have been with you for a long time, or that they will combine into broader, more liberal desires, such as the wish to be happy whatever else happens. Take some time to think this through.

4   Now ask yourself one final question: do you want to be the kind of person who has this wish? Many wishes are generated by our desires to impress, influence and attract others. Is this alright with you? Would you really rather give up some desires?

become lethargic and drift, and make you feel you are losing control of your life.

Take time out to think through your lifestyle. Notice where there is default decision-making and ask yourself if you are happy with it. Ask yourself which of your decisions are made by habit and which are arrived at by conscious reasoning? Are you happy with this state of affairs?

Do you need to take some time out to plan your life a little better? Of course you can't plan happiness but you can plan your life so that it is full of challenges, rewards and comforts which ultimately are the things that bring us happiness. Try having some goals in your life.

THE SOLE GETTER - THE GOAL SETTER

Once you have really made sure of your desires you can start to set yourself goals to actually achieve them. One of the best ways to do this is with friends. Try to find a couple of friends with whom you could meet up on a regular basis.

Start by getting together and listing your wishes in terms of goals. Let each person take their turn to talk and think through how and what they want to attain. Make each person set some short-term goals, e.g. to be achieved in the next three months, some mid-term goals, e.g. to be achieved in the next six to eighteen months, and some long-term goals for the next five years. Meet up with your friends every three or four weeks to encourage each other and see how everyone is progressing.

Setting targets and goals for yourself, as long as they are realistic, can really help to give you a purpose when you might otherwise be feeling low. Make sure your goals are achievable and challenging. Think about an effective way to achieve them, and try to stay faithful to your plans for at least three months.

Staying in mental control

While you are working towards your goals, make sure you stay calm. Don't forget that constant worrying about objectives and targets all the time will only increase pressure. Try to let go, in your mind, of the mental labelling we all go through: 'this is a bad day', 'this is a horrid person', 'this is a wrong move'. Don't tell yourself you're a fool or a hopeless case. If you talk like that you will be! When you find yourself lapsing into this habit, consciously slow down the voice in your head and 'look' at it. Speed the voice up, make it louder, sharper – anything to get control of it – and then banish any negative naggers!

Don't tell yourself: "Help! I'm nervous", or "Oh, I'm so depressed." Acknowledge that there may be elements in your life that you are not happy with, or situations you are not dealing with well, and break things down into manageable chunks. Start to take control of your life with the methods described above and don't lump the whole situation together under one negative heading.

TIME MANAGEMENT

Making things more manageable is not only done in the mind; it can also be useful to look at how you use your time. One of the things time management courses always look at is how and to which projects you devote your time. Many people end up allocating a larger amount of time to small jobs and not enough time to the really important tasks. This could be true of you whether you work in an office environment or not.

Think about your daily schedule and decide which are the really important tasks that need to be done. It is usually only about twenty per cent of tasks that are very important. However, it is usually these tasks that get delayed.

Ask yourself why you are procrastinating? Is it because the job is too difficult? Or too long-winded?

CLEARING THE BLUES
Use some of the methods described above and the ones under the heading of decision-making (page 81), and next time you start to feel depressed stop the feeling creeping up on you and enveloping you in a dull cloud. Take out that sheet of paper and write down everything that is worrying you. Get it out in the open! Use the decision and goal-making process to analyse and formulate a plan that will help you deal with what is getting you down. This may not solve your problems but it will make things more manageable in your own mind and stop the depressive cloud overwhelming you.

Do you feel that you really cannot do the task or is it that you simply have difficulty getting started?

DO IT NOW

One of the times people procrastinate the most is when there is a decision to be made before dealing with an issue. It might be that you haven't quite decided whether to return a faulty product to a shop or you can't make up your mind on which builder to use for a job.

The trouble is that lack of decision means that each time you remember to complete the task you also say, "Oh! but I can't do that yet because I haven't quite made up my mind."

Buy yourself a packet of red stickers! Each time you pick up a form or bill that you haven't made a decision on, or each time you run over it in your mind, stick a red dot on to a sheet of paper. Take a look at that piece of paper in a couple of days. How many red dots are on it?

This will help you to realise how much mental

FOCUSING TOWARDS MEDITATION

As you improve your powers of concentration, you can begin to use them in new ways and to open your mind, and body, to new areas of discovery. Meditation is a very popular topic but there are an amazingly few people who regard this as a real option for life improvement or even relaxation. Do not be put off by the pictures you see of people sitting in cross-legged poses, or by the fact that it is an Eastern philosophy. Meditation does not mean withdrawing from the world but regarding it, perhaps, in a different way. In the next chapter, you will be introduced to various aspects of the meditative concept, but first use your new powers of focusing attention to become still.

Sit in any comfortable position but with your spine straight. For this you may need to focus on your spine to begin with. Or you may need to keep a mental check on your body so that is does not allow the spine to curve. Let go of any tension in the shoulders by allowing them to drop down and widen.

Use your breathing, as in previous exercises (see page 66) to slow your mind. Let thoughts run across the mind but do not follow them. Now close your eyes and keep the same feeling going. You are not meditating but you are learning to put the body into a

position and the mind into a frame where it can begin to make its own journey. Stay like this for a few moments. Try this consecutively for five days and lengthen the period of stillness progressively. Turn to the next chapter to take things further.

(and probably) physical energy you have wasted just thinking about this issue and then putting it 'away' again. without actually dealing with it! If there are more than two red dots on the paper, then probably in the time you have wasted you could have made a decision and dealt with the whole issue – or at least made a start! Be strict with yourself and tell yourself every so often: do it now!

Concentration

The most important factor in achieving any kind of task is concentration. If you want to finish that great novel, get your document typed up or build a perfect sand castle, you will work much better if you do it with full concentration.

Remember that getting started is half the battle so if it's a writing project, pick up that pen and start writing! The mere act of writing can trigger the brain to get going in the right direction. If you're not quite sure how to begin, start anyway, even if it's bang in the middle, and you will find your way.

FAKE CONCENTRATION

Once you have started your task, fake concentration! Even if you don't feel it, make yourself look as though you are concentrating. Imagine you are on TV and act like you are concentrating very hard! People who are intent on their task don't give in to outside distractions and are usually fairly still or move with the minimum of fuss. Each time your mind wanders pull it back to the task in hand.

MAINTAIN CONCENTRATION

This is a little harder than faking it! Once you have begun your task you will still reach a point at which your mind begins to tire. If you reach this point it is best to listen to your body and mind.

If you are doing something physical and you are tiring, take a break. Stop, have a drink of water, stretch, change your view, eat something small. If you have been doing something sedentary, it can really help to move around.

● Get up from your seat, walk about. Face each corner of the room in turn and take a deep breath in and out to each wall. Now reach up both your arms towards the ceiling, stretching through the spine and making yourself as long as you can. Gently drop the head back just slightly looking up at the ceiling as you take the arms back and out to the sides.

● Now drop the chin forwards as the arms come around in front of the body to lead the forward curl. Let the whole body gently curl all the way forwards, leading the arms and head but keeping the weight firmly on the feet.

● When your hands are near to the ground,

STAY RELAXED
Keep a check on your physical posture – stay relaxed but don't allow yourself to fidget or slump too much. Ease yourself in to the task and then you can make slight adjustments so your body remains comfortable. If you have trouble concentrating on what someone is saying, assume the position a focused person might adopt. Doing this, you may find you are really listening.

make sure the knees are slightly bent and rest there momentarily, letting the blood flow towards the brain. Now slowly reverse the curling process so that you uncurl, slowly, through the spine with the head coming last.

● Curling in this way will release the spine and refresh the brain with blood, while the slow uncurl will prevent dizziness.

● Periodically while you are working at your task give yourself a mental prod. Shout in your mind: "Where am I now? What is happening?" Take a look around you and make sure you really see your surroundings. Make sure you can hear what someone is saying and that you understand what is going on. Become aware of the temperature, of the weather outside and of the objects around you. Whenever you feel yourself drifting, shout inside your head: "Where am I now?"

YOUR DIET

Your diet also plays an important part in maintaining concentration. What you eat and when you eat can greatly affect your ability to concentrate. Here are a few basic guidelines:

● If you leave too long a gap between meals, you will find that your mind will become easily distracted. Your brain is like the muscles in your body: it needs fuel, so don't deprive it of food – keep it regularly topped up with good-quality calories.

● Don't eat great big, heavy meals. Even if your work is not physical, a large meal will divert too much blood to the stomach and, again, the brain will be deprived. Small regular meals are advisable

Be good to yourself and increase your ability to concentrate by eating highly nutritious food. Drink plenty of fluids and eat lots of raw fruit and vegetables.

if you know that you need to concentrate.

● Try to eat vegetables, fruits, pasta and bread during the day. These are slow-release carbohydrates which will keep your energy topped up over an extended period unlike sugary foods which give you a 'quick fix' but do not release energy gradually in a controlled way.

IMPROVING YOUR CONCENTRATION

Try the following mind exercises to give yourself a mental work-out!

1   **Take a note!**

Look around your room now and see how many square shapes you can see. Look at the patterns in your fabric, look at the shapes of objects you own and look at the cracks and surfaces of the walls or any natural manifestations. Can you see things you didn't notice before? Or are you aware of how squares make up objects in a way you never realised? This is a very simple example of how you can increase your general awareness.

Try the same idea but with a word. Learn a new word and look for an opportunity to use it. You will be amazed at how quickly you can introduce it into conversation or even how often you now hear this word spoken! Once you become aware of things they start to exist in your consciousness and make a difference to your life for the first time!

2   **Take a number!**

- Recite: 2, 4, 6 and so on up to 100 – easy!
- Now try a double number series: 2,3 4,6 6,9 and so on up to 50 – harder!
- Now try and recite: a double number series with one series going up and one going down: down by 5, up by 4: 100,4 95,8 90,12 etc.

There are many good variations on this theme which you might like to try. With practice you can get really snappy!

3   **Memorize this verse!**

Swan swam over the sea

Swim swan swim

Swan swam back again

Well swam swan!

- Try reciting this verse, line by line, backwards.
- Try reciting this verse in numbers (the numbers corresponding to the number of letters in each word).
- Try reciting this verse omitting every fourth word.

4   **Lateral thinking!**

Bill meets an old friend of his whilst visiting his old home town.

"Hi Bill !" says the friend. "How are you?"

After brief reintroductions, the old friend says, "I'm married to someone you wouldn't know and this is my daughter."

"What is your name?" asks Bill.

"My name is the same as my mother's," the girl replies.

"Then I know your name must be Sarah," says Bill.

How did he know?

This lateral thinker not only makes you look for other possibilities but it also challenges our common assumptions. Why did you assume Bill's friend must be a man? (Or maybe you didn't!) Are there other daily issues and assumptions that you could challenge in your daily life? It might sharpen your mind and bring new ideas into clearer focus.

Note: the answer is that Bill's friend is the mother of the child, also called Sarah.

- Avoid eating too many sweets and chocolates. These will cause sugar and insulin levels to swing from one extreme to another, promoting a false hunger as well as stress-style symptoms.

- Try sucking something sharp, like a lemon, or nibbling on a piece of ginger to awaken your taste buds and your brain!

- Make sure that you always work with a bottle of water beside you. Take frequent sips so that you stay well hydrated throughout the day.

Relaxing the mind

chapter five

ONE OF THE BEST ways of relaxing the mind is meditation. Most people are aware of the practice, but few Westerners really know what it involves and what benefits can be gained. Meditation is another way of releasing the mind from its everyday preoccupations with trivia and routine administration. It can teach you to take a step backwards from your roller coaster ride of life and look inwards to find a new kind of perspective. However, in the Western world, there are many misconceptions about meditation: for instance, many people think of it as a mode of doing nothing – a kind of trance or hypnotic-like state. Others have the idea that meditation is when people mull over their problems, or that it is a religious practice. An attainable goal of meditation is gaining a state of awareness where the mind is free of thoughts and worries. Now doesn't that sound attractive?

Why meditate?

Like the other methods suggested in this book, meditation can help you to relieve tension and stress and even guard against stress-related symptoms, such as hypertension, migraines and insomnia. However, when practised on a regular basis, it can also take you one stage further. How many times have you wondered if, and how, you can change yourself? It might be that you feel you need to relax more or that you need to become more tolerant, but do you know how to approach these changes?

The process of meditation can be likened to taking off several layers of clothes in the heat of the sun. With every layer that is removed, so are old habits, clichéd beliefs and thoughtless conditioning. As you pull away layers of clothing to expose the flesh underneath, you see yourself, your values and your relationships to other people and the world more clearly. Meditation, then, takes a holistic approach, i.e. involving both the mind and body. By turning your attention inwards you can become familiar with your innermost thoughts and feelings. By being more in touch with yourself, you have a greater control over your own personality and therefore the quality of your own life.

You may discover that as you develop a new kind of awareness, sensations become more vivid, your ability to concentrate increases and creativity is enhanced. Suddenly you will find that you start to rely on your own judgements, not those of others; that you will look to yourself, and not to other people for approval. This all helps you to cope better with everyday pressures; to adapt to new environments more quickly; and to generally increase your mental and physical wellbeing.

WHAT IS MEDITATION?

Meditation is more a state of mind than a specific activity. It is the conscious desire and effort to calm the mind and look inwards at yourself rather than outwards at the world. This is not a selfish, egocentric look inwards but it is a genuine curiosity about your own personality and a desire for self improvement. Thus meditation will benefit others as well as you!

It can take many different forms including the following: prayer and performing rituals to calm the body and mind, using mantras and sounds to still the mind, and listening to music. It can also be a walk in the countryside, a sport or leisure pursuit or even having a bath! All these things and many more can be forms of meditation if the mind is engaged in the right way. Practising relaxation with full concentration and awareness is one thing; lying on the floor and planning tomorrow's schedule is quite different.

Absorption into your thinking can bring about a meditative state of mind, which is why some sports that require deep concentration can be meditative, as can that state between consciousness and sleeping when the mind has just begun to let go of all its thoughts as it prepares the body for sleep.

Meditation can be practised as an activity, as well as a state of mind: the act of stilling the body and letting go of the mind. Initially, these things will take concerted effort and application and can be as much of a challenge as learning to ski! In Western society, learning to be still is as difficult and alien as learning a new kind of movement.

The two-minute mental mountain

● How easy is it for you to really clear your mind and for more than a few seconds, and give yourself a mental breather from all those myriad thoughts and worries that fill you every day?

Find a watch with a second hand or a digital counter on it and time two minutes. As you look at the watch try not to think of anything for those two minutes. Concentrate on not following your thoughts but only registering them. If you find your mind travelling after a thought, stop the watch. Try not to think about anything.

How did you do? Did you make it to a minute, thirty seconds or even five seconds? This may prove a more difficult exercise than you expected it to be. However, it may make you more aware of just how much of the time your mind tends to run with thoughts of which you don't even take any notice. Meditative practices, if performed on a regular basis, will go some way towards slowing down both your mind and body so that you can concentrate on deeper thoughts and feelings.

TRY THE SHAVASANA MEDITATION POSITION

Lie on the floor with legs apart and relaxed so that your knees and hips are opened out. Your arms are out to the sides of the body, and your head is resting on the floor. Just lie there for a few moments and see if you can keep the body absolutely still without becoming rigid with tension. Try to stay still for up to three minutes. If you find yourself becoming tense or fidgety, stop and try again another time. With practice, your ability to become still will gradually improve.

Now try a mental version of the form of meditation described above (the two-minute mental mountain).

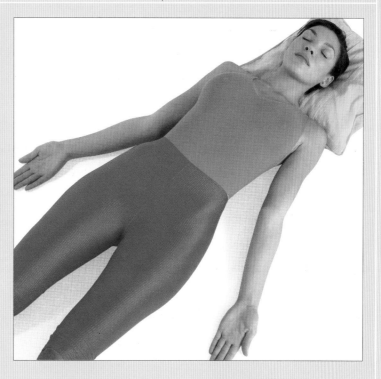

In the mood

When you decide to try some form of meditation, think about where you might do it. Choose a place where you can have some privacy – interruptions are not helpful to a non-thinking state of mind! Find a place that is warm enough if you choose a non-moving form of meditation, and wear comfortable clothing. Cotton and silk are natural, non-restrictive materials, or you might have a favourite top you wear when it is your day off or 'time out'. If so, wear this and it will remind you of making time for you and your inner self.

Try to have some relaxing lighting, not bright overhead fluorescents but perhaps some candles or low lamplight. Scented candles or incense burners might also help you to get in the mood.

Getting in the mood is really just a way of acclimatizing your mind and body to what you are about to do: slowing yourself down and preparing yourself for some time to relax.

WHEN?

Different times of the day may suit different people depending on lifestyle, work commitments, time of year etc. It is not essential to put aside a set time of day, but most people find this easiest when establishing the practice. Otherwise you may well find that time trickles away and still you haven't got around to doing it. Try not to become obsessive about making time, but initially you may have to remind yourself to meditate; like everything else, it takes time to establish a routine. As the old adage goes, it takes twenty one days to form a habit!

Avoid meditating after a meal – you are less likely to be alert as your blood is diverted to the stomach for digestion. This may even cause drowsiness, but remember that although the mind is supposed to be calmed, it must also be attentive.

POSTURE

There are many positions in which to attempt the meditative state of mind. They range from the advanced yogic position called the lotus to any comfortable position in which you can get your mind and body to become still.

If you are interested in reading further about this subject, you will find information on all stages of sitting posture in both the Indian and Chinese teachings, such as the 'perfect posture' (siddhasana) or the 'easy posture' and the 'pose of attainment'. Try for yourself the half lotus position (opposite) once you have established your meditation sessions.

WAYS OF MEDITATING

Once you have calmed yourself and are in the right frame of mind to attempt some kind of meditation, then you have to decide on which technique to use. There are no right or wrong ways of meditating; it comes down to purely personal preference and finding the technique that suits you best. If you are a very active person who finds it difficult to concentrate when still, it might be that some form of Yoga or Tai Chi would be best for you. However, if you need something very still to focus you, it might be that sitting, closing your eyes and focusing on your breath will suit you better. Overleaf are various techniques of meditation that you might like to try. The ones featured here are just a few popular examples, but there are many other ways of getting into meditation which you may discover if you take the time to find out about them.

HALF LOTUS POSITION

1   Use this position for meditation. First limber up your legs by sitting on the floor with knees bent and the soles of your feet together. With hands behind you on the floor for support, gently press your knees towards the floor and release them. Repeat 4 or 5 times.

2   In the same position as above, except that you are now holding on to your ankles, press forwards, lowering your face towards the feet as close as you can. Return to the upright position and repeat several more times until the hip joints feel a little looser.

3   Now for the half lotus: sit on the floor with both legs outstretched. Bend the left leg bringing the left foot beneath the right thigh, as close as possible to the buttocks. Now bend the right knee and place the right foot on top of the left thigh. Both knees should touch the ground which gives a good balanced and stable position for meditation.

● This is a relatively easy position to maintain and, surprisingly it is also remarkably comfortable as it keeps the back straight whilst leaving it feeling very well supported.

BREATH AWARENESS

Breathing has been mentioned many times in this book, and this just illustrates how fundamental it is to both mind and body relaxation. The relationship between our breath and our mental and physical states shows that breath control can be used to induce specific outlooks and an improvement in our general state of health.

Breathing is not only used for stress management, endurance fitness training and Yoga (another meditative practice) but also to cleanse and still the mind. In terms of meditation, breathing techniques are probably one of the most accessible and simple ways of working inwards. Breathing is a process that unites us all: it is non-religious and non-controversial; we all need to breathe and we all can become aware of our breath if we meditate and put our minds to it (right).

MANTRAS

These are another technique for meditating. Sound, rather like the breath, is universal. It has the power to produce different states in different people, and also the power to mesmerize and absorb the mind. Many religions and mystical practices recognise the influence of sound, and from this some great traditions have evolved. These range from hymn singing in school assemblies to chanted

Opposite: when you become aware of your breathing, you can start on the journey inwards to self-discovery. Try one of the awareness meditation techniques.

BREATH AWARENESS MEDITATION

Try any one of the following three techniques to introduce you to the art of breath awareness meditation.

1 **Sit in your chosen position, e.g. half lotus, and make yourself comfortable. Close your eyes or lower your eyelids. Breathe naturally. Start to count your breaths on either the inhalation or exhalation from one to ten. As you find your thoughts drifting, just bring your attention back to the numbers. If you lose count, begin again. If you reach ten, start from one. Try to let the thoughts and feelings just come and go. As you begin to really focus you will realise just how different this process is from just sitting and day dreaming. It takes a concentrated and alert mind.**

2 **Sitting as before, breathe naturally. Begin to focus your attention on the tip of your nostrils where the breath flows in and out of the body. Feel the sensation at the tip of the nostrils and focus on this. Bring back your wandering attention gently.**

3 **Sitting as before, while breathing naturally, start to concentrate on the space between breaths: the space outside the body where the exhalation ends and the space inside the body where the inhalation ends. At these points, notice the stillness. Bring your attention back each time it wanders and keep focusing on the stillness of breath. Eventually, this will also bring a stillness of mind. With practice, you will find that the spaces between the breaths increase.**

Note: You might like to try combining these breathing techniques with the sitting postures already described (see page 94).

prayers, and even to the morale-boosting chants of a football crowd or the haka of the New Zealand rugby team!

CHOOSING A MANTRA

You can choose any phrase or word, meaningless or otherwise. It stands to reason that repeating something pleasant or calming might help to induce a relaxed mood. Don't pick a word or phrase with sad or disappointing connotations. Some people pick religious phrases or an Indian mantra such as: 'Om namah shivaya' (I bow to Shiva; the self).

Others might use any name for God, and so on. Once you have decided on a mantra that you like, stick with it so that it becomes associated with your meditative practice, and a gateway to mind stillness.

Meditating with a mantra

Sit comfortably in an upright position with eyes closed or half closed. Repeat your mantra silently, slowly at first, and then at your normal speaking speed. Become absorbed in the saying and repeating of the word. Focus your attention on this. Keep your attention aware but focused. As your mind becomes still you can stop repeating the mantra, but keep the mind focused on it. If your thoughts wander, return to the repetition to quieten the mind.

There are many variations on meditating with mantras and you may wish to go on to further study if you find this technique works well for you.

VISUAL MEDITATION

This involves actually looking at an object in order to focus the mind and the attention. By gazing at the object and then trying to visualize, the

Sit in a darkened room with a lighted candle in front of you. Gaze at the candle for several seconds and then close your eyes. You will find the image still shining on the back of your forehead as you look at the darkness behind your eyes. However, this image may be only momentary and then it may start to fade.

How clearly now can you see the detail of that candle. Can you see the exact formation of the wax? Can you see the true colours of the flame? Can you still hold the true image in front of you?

It is, in fact, very difficult to hold a precise mental picture, and it takes time and practice to acquire this skill. When you start performing this exercise, you might find that you spend more time with your eyes open observing the candle than with your eyes closed, visualizing. Don't worry if this happens to you; with time and practice, you will be able to improve your ability to retain a mental picture steadily.

mind is kept aware but stilled in its concentration.

The images used in visual meditative practices vary greatly. They may be paintings and carvings of Christ from orthodox churches, or mystical diagrams, such as those used in the East in Buddhist or Hindu traditions. There are also the beautiful and complex mandalas of the tantric Yoga which are designed to guide the attention inwards and to increase spiritual development.

Mandalas and other complicated art forms are advanced forms of visual meditation. When you decide to try this practice, you can start with a simpler method, as outlined above.

Close your eyes and then try to visualize your chosen object in detail, e.g. a lighted candle.

Other visualization exercises

Try these other exercises to help you to practise visualization techniques.

1 Rather than using a darkened room and a candle, create a black spot in a bright room. Paint one on a large piece of paper and pin it to the wall. Sit comfortably in one of the recommended sitting positions, if possible, and try to concentrate your entire attention on the spot.

The useful thing about a black dot is that it is abstract and therefore should have no connotations. This is advantageous when starting out because it prevents the mind slipping away. If you were to use a cup as you focus, for example, you might be tempted to think about what it is made of, where it came from, what it holds in it etc. The black dot will help you to avoid being distracted.

2 Try concentrating your gaze on the end of your nose; although this is hard on the eyes, it breaks the tendency to bring other objects around you into focus. It is also an almost physical representation of the mental attitude you should have when approaching meditation.

3 If you find the above exercise too difficult, then try closing the eyes and focusing on the point between the eyebrows on the inside of your head. This eliminates all outside visual stimuli, but you must still concentrate on keeping the thoughts intent on the inner picture.

CHOOSING A VISUAL IMAGE

As mentioned above, a simple object, such as a lighted candle, can be used initially. Once you have

OTHER IMAGES
Another approach is to gaze at a written word or even a written sound. Gazing at calligraphy, for instance, or even letters, or the symbol of the word 'OM' can all be methods of visual meditation.

TO PRACTISE VISUAL MEDITATION
Sit comfortably in a seated position. Place the object you have chosen one to two metres away from you at eye level. Look at the object and try to become absorbed in the looking and seeing, not in what the object is about. After a few moments, close your eyes and try to visualize the object for as long as possible. If the image disappears or becomes unclear, open your eyes and repeat the process. With practice, your mental image will become clearer until you will no longer need the original object.

Allow your thoughts to come and go but don't let them lead you away from your visualization of the object.

become more proficient in this, you may want to progress to other images. There are a myriad of symbols you can choose. The fourth-century Buddhist text lists ten different subjects, ranging from the elements – earth, fire, water and air – to colours – blue, yellow, red and white – and light and space. Natural objects, such as a stone or a blade of grass, can be good subjects or you can even try the Tao idea of watching the moving clouds.

There are also many mystic and religious symbols that are very popular. For instance, the Yin-yang one which symbolizes opposites, such as light and dark, night and day, masculine and feminine, and the negative and positive poles of Tai Chi. Other well known symbols you can use include the cosmic egg (the seed of life) picture or the serpent (a latent spiritual energy) picture.

FOCUSING TECHNIQUES

Concentration is a powerful tool of meditation and there are many other exercises that you can try in order to improve it. Start off with an exercise to eliminate objects.

1   Take four objects: they could be anything, e.g. a cup and saucer with a spoon placed on a table. Sit comfortably and start by gazing at all the objects and trying to memorize precisely the details and position of each object. Now close your eyes and try to eliminate the objects in your vision, one by one. Start with the table, then the saucer, and then the spoon until you have the cup left in mid air and eventually you eliminate it.

2   Now try exercising the right and left hemispheres of the brain. Focus your attention on the left hemisphere, and picture a high mountain cave. Now concentrate on the right hemisphere, and picture a young girl playing a violin. Develop the right image first and fix this in your brain, then the left.

3   Now picture the figure of a hermit Yogi emerging from the cave enchanted by the sounds of the violin. In your other hemisphere, the girl stops playing her violin and walks towards the old man. Picture both figures slowly advancing towards each other; the hermit Yogi in his flowing robes and the young girl carrying her instrument, both smiling at one another.

This exercise acknowledges the differences between the right hemisphere of the brain with its artistic and musical tendencies, and the more verbal and analytical hemisphere of the left.

4   This is an exercise in concentrating on an idea. Here are a few suggestions for meditation ideas. Start by sitting comfortably on a soft surface and contemplate the body as though it is unsupported and weightless. Contemplate the idea of this, not the feelings, such as 'it might feel like flying', or a similar situation, e.g. 'I could be in a space craft'. Try not to fantasize – just keep your mind focused on the idea on weightlessness.

Contemplate the skin covering your body as an empty shell. Focus on the emptiness inside you. Bring your mind back to this subject each time it starts to wander.

Contemplate the following question: what is health? Think this question through and retain your attention until you can realise a considered point of view. This may take practice because concentrating on an idea is harder then concentrating on an object, but it will develop in time.

Note: all meditative concentration will help you to bring your focus inwards and, for a while, let the flow and tumble of your normal thoughts run by unheeded. You should emerge from a meditation session feeling refreshed and rested without feeling drowsy. Try to let go of your meditative state of mind slowly; you will lose many of the benefits if you jump from a restful frame of find to another more active one too quickly. Sit or lie down for a few minutes, adjusting mentally. Stretch your muscles gently, then take some deep breaths and look around you.

Active meditation

Meditation does not have to be inactive or sedentary; some forms can be active and even athletic. Any physical activity pursued in the right way can give rise to meditative thought but there are also some techniques that derive from ancient traditions and which are famous for both their thoughtful and their active qualities.

Tai Chi Chuan

This is probably one of the best known soft martial arts. It is labelled the art of awareness. Derived from the oldest Tao principles, its symbol refers to the polarity of opposites: light and dark, yin and yang etc. 'Chuan' means 'the fist way'.

Tai Chi works on the principle of a constant flow of spherical movement which enhances energy and circulates it around the body. Practitioners claim that regular practice prevents the onset of illness, and when the Chinese authorities carried out a survey they found that regular practitioners of the 'Short form' had significantly more efficient circulatory and respiratory systems and metabolism.

Tai Chi is also a form of spiritual or meditation training. You have to concentrate totally on the movements while you are making them, and this helps calm the mind and can induce a feeling of well-being and equilibrium. Tai Chi has been dubbed the 'moving meditation', as the movements require an emptying of the mind, letting go of feelings and intentions. Over time, this can develop a sense of detachment but with its own rhythm.

Tan Tien

Below are some basic stances for Tai Chi movement. Try these and if you feel that this type of meditation would suit you, then look for books or videos on the subject to give you a basic philosophy of the art before you begin to practise seriously.

According to the Chinese, Chi (a part of several martial arts) has a centre in the body known as Tan Tien. This area is the body's centre of gravity and for every movement of the limbs there is a natural counterbalancing movement, which is always felt at the Tan Tien from which, it is said, all movement originates. Try this deep breathing exercise to get in touch with your Tan Tien.

● Stand in a relaxed stance with your mouth closed. Place your hands over your stomach about 5cm/2 inches below the navel so that you can feel the Tan Tien moving with you as you breathe. Inhale deeply through your nose, letting the abdomen fill gently. Breathe slowly and deeply without extra effort or noise.

Exhale through the nose from the Tan Tien until you are empty of air. Try to breathe in this way for approximately five minutes and, as your concentration develops, think about the vital energy travelling in a circular motion from the nose to the lungs and to the Tan Tien, then up and out again, never stopping.

Tai Chi walking

This is a basic method of foot movements and weight transfer which is a good way for a beginner to absorb the correct posture and rhythm of the movements. Once you have learned the rhythms you can practise the Short form which is a sequence of flowing movements divided into twenty four steps and one of the best known Tai Chi exercises.

1 The take up posture: stand with heels together and toes turned out slightly. Breathe from the Tan Tien. Feel the weight in your feet and place your hands lightly on your hips. Bend the knees softly.

2 Move your left foot forwards and outwards as if you were skating on ice. Place the left heel on the ground but keep the weight on the right leg. Gaze ahead of you.

3 Now transfer the weight into the left leg as you press the toe down. Keep the knees over the toes as the left knee is slightly bent and the right leg straightens. Raise your right foot to bring the legs together, keeping the heel up.

4 Keep moving the right leg forwards and out to the right to place the right heel on the ground, and then repeat the movements with the other leg leading. Move at a smooth, even pace with no bobbing of the head or the shoulders.

● Even as you are performing this simple beginners' exercise, you can begin to feel some of the rhythm and philosophy of Tai Chi. As your body keeps moving, so the energy keeps flowing and each preceding move adds more power to the succeeding moves.

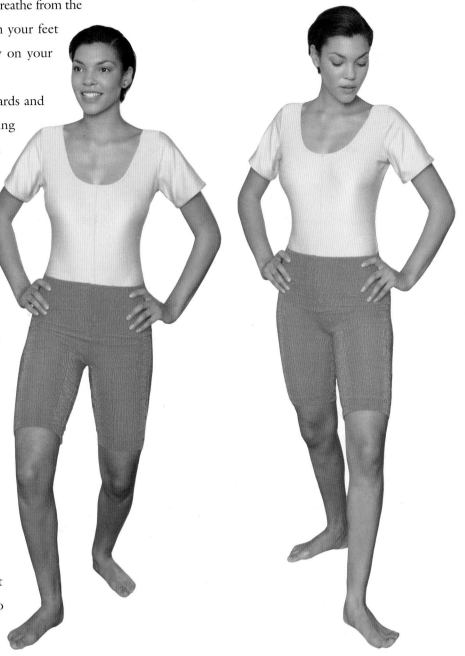

Yoga

This looks inwards, as do most Eastern philosophies, for a release from materialistic anxiety and for a fulfilment of purpose which integrates the self into the world as a cosmic whole.

Hatha Yoga is still the best known, and the more physical, form of Yoga. It is another kind of movement which must be performed with complete concentration and involvement. Again, the emphasis is on natural and slow movements so that each different position in a sequence is expressed, and no movements are strained or go against the natural alignment of the body. Good Yoga teachers will not emphasise some of the extreme ending positions which can only be achieved over some time with practice. However, they will allow the student to progress at his or her own pace with no 'goal' to be achieved, apart form the feeling of well-being.

SOME TIPS FOR YOGA MOVEMENT

● Move slowly and with intention so that you become aware of the whole body and the part it plays in moving your limbs and torso.

FRONT PUSH UP

1 Start on all-fours with elbows soft, not locked.

2 Tuck the toes underneath you and lift the knees off the floor as you push your backside into the air. Let the head hang down. Hold for a count of 5.

3 A variation here is to press the heels back towards the floor so that you also feel a stretch up the back of the legs.

4 Now slowly bend the knees until you replace them on the floor. As you rest in this all-fours position, again keep the head in line with the rest of the spine.

5 Repeat from step 2 twice more and then drop the knees right down, with the head resting on the floor to recover.

● Make sure there is no strain in any of these movements and if you find holding for a count of 5 is too long to begin with, then only hold momentarily. You will build up strength with regular practice. Remember to keep the mind on your body and don't allow outside thoughts to distract you.

Yoga is not about forcing the body into unusual positions but about a journey in movement, without force, so that the improvements come from inside your own body. Try these basic moves to see if this might be the kind of moving meditation that works for you.

Note: as you continue to practise Yoga, you will find that you will achieve increased sensitivity and awareness of both your mind and body, and tension and anxiety will start to decrease. Practise your Yoga positions with some of the breathing exercises suggested in other chapters.

● When you feel you have gone far enough in any Yoga combination, concentrate on the particular body parts involved in the move. This will ensure that you are using the right muscles to a maximum and will help focus the mind.

● Slow deliberate movement will help strengthen the body and calm the mind.

THE COIL

1 Lie on your back on the floor with arms and legs straight and together. Rest the palms of the hands on the floor.

2 Gently bend the knees and, keeping the legs together, bring then in as close to your chest as you possibly can.

3 Link the hands and loop them over the knees Breathe in.

4 Pull in on the knees and press your nose towards them as you exhale; you will feel a release of pressure in the back. Hold this position for the count of 5. Holding positions will help to increase bodily strength and flexibility. Mental concentration must be maintained in these held positions if breathing is to be kept regular and natural.

5 Lower the head to the floor and relax like this for a few seconds.

6 Repeat the movement from step 4 twice more.

7 Finally return to the original starting position and from there start to relax.

Dance meditation

There are many different forms of dance and some are specifically ritual or meditational. Any kind of dance can be appropriate, however, as long as it is performed with an absorbed state of mind. Much of the time, dance, in our Western society, is a very self-conscious tradition. We dance in discos and other social venues where we are conscious of onlookers and people judging us as if it were a competition. Or we watch dance as an exhibition of skill, a contrived art form with often very extreme forms of bodily misalignment, such as ballet. Dance meditation, then, has to be natural, emanating from inside yourself so that you connect to your own inner self and no-one else's.

Wear loose clothing so that you are uninhibited, and find somewhere private where you have space to move. Put on some music that you particularly like and that really makes you want to move. This is the most natural way to get your body moving if you allow the sounds to really rock you. Find some sounds – they don't have to be tuneful – that can allow you to express different aspects of yourself. The sounds might begin with an energetic beat that gets you leaping and jumping around or they might start with some gentle lilting tunes that start you off rocking on your feet, and which build gradually into flowing, undulating movements.

You will discover that dancing in this way will increase your muscle tone and endurance. You will also find a new vitality as you focus your mind and release tension and worries through your movement. There are many formal dance techniques available for you to learn if you wish to take this form of 'meditation' further.

'Dance of letting go'

Now start to move around to the music in any way you want. Don't worry about what you look like, nor if the movements repeat themselves; just move and keep on moving. Use all the parts of your body and just experience the sheer joy of moving in any way you feel like. Use the music or ignore the music, turn it up loud or stamp it out as you move with abandon and listen to your own inner rhythm!

Like every other form of meditation, regular practice can help you to get more out of a technique. Dancing with abandon and until the point where you lose your inhibitions may take some practice. It will also take some time before you learn how to keep going.

'Dance of improvisation'

Try dancing for extended periods. Start with two minutes and build towards fifteen minutes. As you begin to extend your sessions, you may find you are running out of ideas. Here are some tips to keep you dancing!

● Dance in any way but face each different corner of the room.

● Move around reaching up as high as you can, using the full stretch of your body. Use the tips of your toes and the extension of your fingers and the lifting through the whole spine to reach into each corner and up as far as you can. Repeat the process, going as low as you can. Find different ways to move around on a low level. Try putting your weight on different body parts as you keep moving with the music.

● Try leading the movement with different parts of your body. Make your elbow lead you everywhere you go, then your knee or your chin. Try any kind of movement that is led by any body part.

● Think about movement you wouldn't normally do. Are you moving very fast? Then start to move slower and even slower again. See how slowly you can move before you stop moving completely! If you always dance while flinging your arms about, try moving and dancing but with your arms relaxed by your sides. By challenging yourself your body will start to find new ways to move.

● Try using your dance to influence your mood. Start to dance as if you are sad. Dance as if you have just received wonderful news. Dance as if you are bored. Notice which movements come from which frame of mind.

Zen meditation

Zazen meditation is known as the sitting meditation associated with the Zen Buddhist tradition. It differs from other techniques already mentioned in that it does not involve focusing the attention on a particular object, such as breath, or a visual image. Instead, it focuses on an opening out of the attention, so that you are conscious of what is happening externally and internally.

Whilst you should be attentive and alert, this practice allows thoughts and feelings to come and go without interference. In Zen meditation, the eyes are usually kept open. Try a Zen-style meditation to see how different it is.

With Zen meditation you can broaden your attitude to include everything, internally and externally.

1 Sit up very straight, either in one of the key sitting positions (see page 95) or on the edge of a hard chair. Clasp the left hand over the right, and rest them in your lap.

2 Sit with your gaze lowered, looking at a spot about a metre away from you, and breathe naturally.

3 Now just rest here without trying to think about anything, but let any thoughts and impressions enter your mind without chasing them away. Don't try to shut out sounds and smells or any phenomena – just be aware of them without judging. You should sit with nothing in mind and no sense of purpose, just your impressions.

Afterwards, move your body slowly; rotate the wrists and ankles and extend your limbs gradually before standing up.

MEDITATION – IS IT FOR YOU?

As we have seen, there are many different forms of meditation and meditative practices available and the only way to find out if meditation suits you is to try it out! Most people will gain something from having a meditative aspect to their lives. However, remember that when you do decide to take the plunge, you must start with a positive attitude and give yourself at least four sessions before you give up! Virtually everything in life takes practice, and this is essential if you are to improve and gain the positive benefits of meditation.

The pleasure principle

chapter six

WE ALL POSSESS the ability to take pleasure in our own minds and bodies, and this is a natural way of relaxing. Massage is one of the great ways to experience the pleasures of the body, and touch can be one of the most relaxing pleasures of all. You recognise sensation when your skin is touched, and you use the power of touch to focus the mind and ease away physical aches and pains. Firm, pressured strokes can release tensions and anxieties, as well as helping you to appreciate the positive feelings you derive from touch. Using aromatic oils can add to this experience and make it more sensual. You will also find some suggestions for using water to relax the body, leaving you revived and refreshed. Finally, sleep. This is nature's great restorer and a relaxer of both the body and the mind.

Massage

Massage is becoming recognised as one of the most beneficial therapies for all kinds of stress symptoms as well as helping to boost blood and lymphatic circulation. It can warm both flesh and muscle, helping to disperse any tightness and also encouraging the release of waste products.

You don't need to be a qualified masseur to apply some basic touching principles. Trust your hands and touch someone else in the way you would like to be touched. Stroking your hands rhythmically and fluidly over the body will relax and warm the muscles, enliven the skin and help boost circulation. Squeezing and kneading, where you lift and press the flesh with one or both hands, will invigorate and release muscular tightness. Pressing sensitively with thumbs and fingers, or the heel of your hand, will add pressure to the muscle to ease away deeper tension, and release toxins from the tissues. Put your strokes together in a flowing manner, so that one motion leads easily into another.

THE THREE FISTS MASSAGE

There are three major areas of tension in the body, and these are sometimes known as the three fists of tension. These areas are: the head and neck, the chest and diaphragm, and the pelvic regions. Use your hands to smooth away tension and blockages in these areas; it will leave you feeling immediately revived!

The first fist

1   Begin with the first fist of tension: the neck and shoulders. Take both hands and press the thumbs and fingertips firmly into the Trapezius, gently squeezing it. This is the muscle that runs down the back of the neck and across the shoulders. Gently exert pressure on the muscle every couple of centimetres until each hand reaches the top of each shoulder.

2   Now begin to work your way back towards the neck with the fingers, making circular movements every few centimetres.

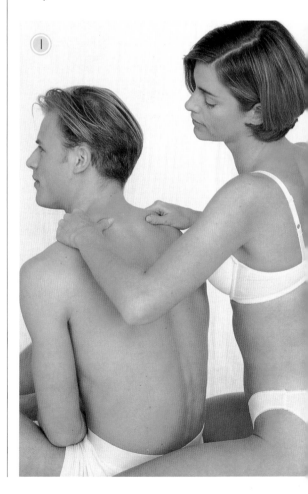

3 At the base of the head, use the first two fingers of each hand to press away tension all around the outline of the skull.

4 Now use all the fingers, working them in circular motions, to massage the back and sides of the scalp underneath the hair, rather as if you were shampooing it. Work your way upwards towards the crown of the head.

5 Finally scrunch your fingertips into the hair tugging it gently away from the scalp. Pull only enough to stimulate the roots. This will leave the head feeling amazingly invigorated!

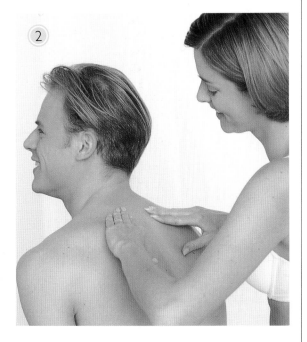

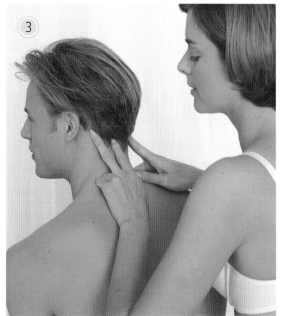

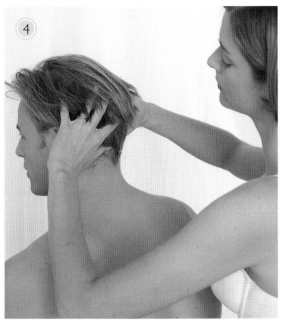

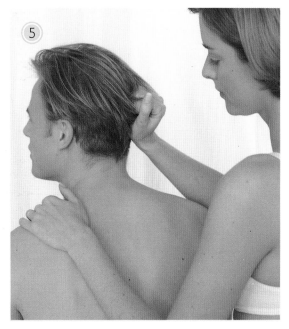

The second fist

1 To release tension in the stomach, diaphragm and belly, start by rubbing the flat of both hands in a clockwise motion over the abdominal area. Start with small circles to cover the areas right down from the bottom of the ribs to the top of the pelvic bone.

2 Now locate your solar plexus; an inch or so down from where the ribs meet. Now take a deep breath and, as you exhale, press the fingers of one hand into the area, gently but steadily.

3 With the outer edge of both hands, press underneath the lower ribcage with the out-breath to release any pent-up tension around the diaphragm.

4 Finally reach alternate hands around the side of your body and sweep the hands back and forth across the navel, massaging and relieving tension from the sides of the abdomen.

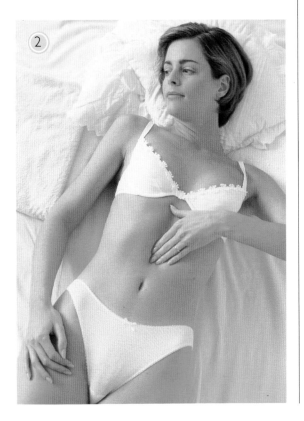

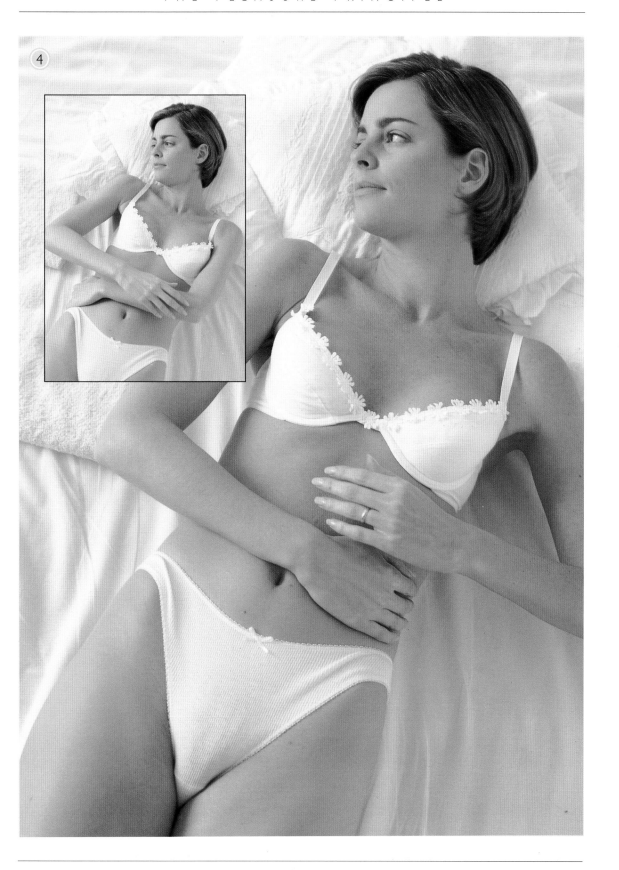

The third fist

Important lymphatic sites are located in the groin between the pelvis and legs, and stroking down from the hip bones and sweeping out into the inner thighs can help stimulate these areas.

1 Stroke from the top of the thighs inwards and upwards over the lymph sites and out to the hips.

2 & 3 Now place your hands on your hips with the thumbs in front and the fingertips behind. Squeeze the fingers and thumbs inwards, firmly, hold and then release. Repeat three or four times to release tension from the back of the pelvis.

4 Finally, turn over on to the front and make several long, firm strokes with the fingertips, starting from the buttocks, up the back and finishing at the bottom of the ribcage.

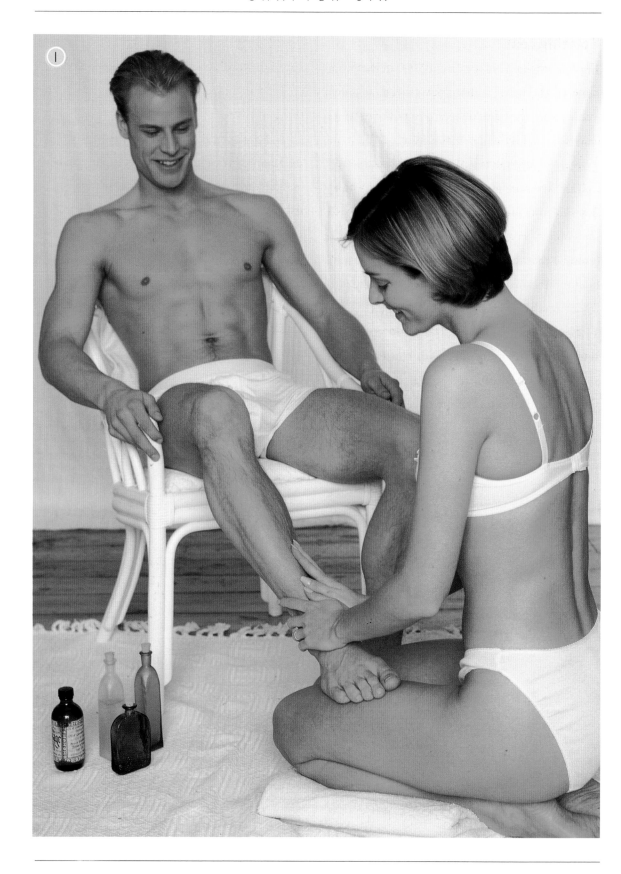

Relaxing foot massage

The feet are also a major source of sensation, and in some therapies, e.g. reflexology or metamorphic technique, the feet are considered to be the route to relaxation points all over the body. Take it in turns to try the routine below with a friend to really feel ease and relaxation from the bottom upwards! Ask your friend to soak his/her feet in a bowl of warm water for up to ten minutes. You could put a blend of essential oils into the water. (See page 121 for an explanation.) Now take his/her feet out of the water and pat them dry.

1 Start to massage your friend's feet gently. Work on one foot at a time. Start by stroking the flat of the hands up and over the foot, around the ankles and back down the sole several times in a steady rhythm.

2 Now place your fingers on top of the foot, and the thumbs beneath. Move each thumb alternately in rapid circular motions, starting from the heel and moving up towards the toes. Press firmly all over the sole. Pay particular attention to the arch of the foot but be sensitive as this is often a tender area.

3 Now press the thumbs steadily on one spot at a time all over the sole. If you feel any tender spots or crystalline deposits, spend a little extra time on this area and then move on.

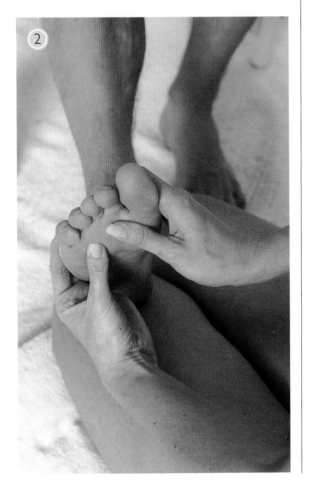

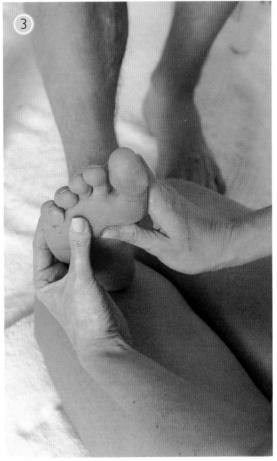

4 Work on the toes now, by using the index fingers to grip each digit firmly and then squeeze gently along each toe. Then stretch the toe by pulling it gently along its length to its tip.

5 Move your fingers to the ankle and make little circular movements around the bones several times.

6 Finish by gently massaging the Achilles tendon at the back of the heel. Gently roll the tendon between your thumb and fingers to give this tendon release and flexibility.

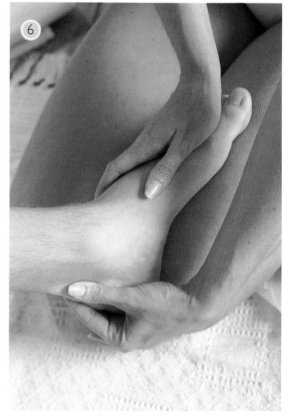

SENSUAL MASSAGE

Your sexuality is an important part of your personality and is also a key to great relaxation! There are many ways of relaxing into your sexuality, and enhancing your sexual awareness and pleasure. Try using the powers of visualization you have

AROMATHERAPY

Aromatherapy is the ancient art of using natural ingredients found in plants, herbs, flowers, fruits and the bark, roots or resin of some trees. The molecules of these natural ingredients are often what give the plant or tree its very special aroma, or ambience, and these are called essential oils. The molecules of these essential oils evaporate very quickly but they also penetrate the human skin and enter the bloodstream and organs quickly too, before eventually being excreted by the body.

Using these oils can enhance your massage treatments and encourage deeper relaxation and recovery. Essential oils are very potent and are usually diluted in a carrier oil. It is in this form that they can be applied directly to the skin. You need the correct dilution so follow the instructions on the aromatherapy pack to make sure that you get it right.

Oils can also be added to bath water or foot baths, used to scent your room or even added to a machine wash for a relaxing smell to your clothes! As a basic starter kit you might like to try buying the following oils: Jasmine, Lavender, Neroli, Peppermint, Sandalwood and Ylang ylang, for insstance.

These oils mix well with others and have a wide range of relaxing uses. For instance, Ylang ylang is good for both stress and circulation problems, whereas Peppermint is beneficial for breathing problems and fatigue.

learned in previous chapters to meditate on this!

Touching and being touched are among the most relaxing options open to all of us. It is a language all of its own and can be a very intimate way of communicating between lovers. Massage can invigorate or relax, producing soporific feelings or replenishing vital energy. Gentle massage with a partner can help to relax both of you and provide a way of easing you both into a more relaxed mood where you are more receptive to touch and to each other, after the intensity and pressures of a busy day.

As most couples work apart, it takes time at the end of a day for both partners to integrate again. It also takes time for us to let the thoughts and worries of the day fall away from us. A whole body massage is a wonderfully sensual experience and can draw the mind away from external distractions and help us to focus on pleasures and sensations within the body. A short period of gentle massage between you and your partner can change your mood, make you forget niggling worries and create a relaxed and intimate atmosphere ready for love-making. By focusing the massage around the belly and pelvis area, you can provide greater sexual relaxation and promote complete trust.

1 Have your partner lie on the bed, in a warm room, unclothed.

2 Get him to bend one knee and lift the right hip so that you can slide your hand between his legs and up behind his back. Place your other hand on top of the stomach and rest it there for a few moments, allowing your hand to warm the skin.

Most water therapies are very relaxing as water is a natural and familiar substance, known to us even before our birth, so it makes sense that it can help to calm us. Water exercise, such as aquarobics or even just gentle swimming up and down your local pool, is a great de-stresser as it not only rests the mind but the water supports your body weight and can relieve aches and tensions.

3   Reach across and hook your hand over his hip and pull it gently towards you so that you are rocking the hips from side to side. Repeat with your other hand beneath and then rock the pelvis to the other side.

4   Replace your hand directly in the middle of the abdomen and ask your partner to direct his breath towards the heat of your touch. Tell him to breathe in and then, on the exhale, send all the breath and energy down towards your waiting hand.

5   Move your hand from one area to another while your partner breathes into each new touch.

6   Now take some oil and spread it over the abdomen, then for some minutes stroke lovingly over the belly, hips and pubic area.

7   Gently turn your partner over and stroke the oil over his back and massage to relax his muscles. Focus on the buttocks, stroking firmly to warm the area. Follow up by kneading the fleshy areas of the buttocks and the sides of the body.

8   Now, using the thumbs, start in the middle of

Opposite: using oils can make a massage a more invigorating, sensual experience. Choose your oils with care to create the desired effect.

the back, pressing on the muscles lining either side of the spine. (Do not press directly on the spine.) Press like this all the way down until you come on to the buttocks. Use your fist to press into the large muscles of the buttocks to release any tension and thereby increase erotic sensation.

9   Finally place your right hand across the coccyx and, positioning your left hand on top of your right, press down gently but steadily with all your body weight so that you extend the spinal curve and relax the back.

Water relaxers

Water is another of the many pleasurable relaxation methods you might like to try. As a form of therapy, water can be very calming and relaxing. We all know how therapeutic a warm bath can be at the end of the day; or how refreshing and invigorating a shower is first thing in the morning. Below are a few suggestions of water therapies you might like to try as a further guide to relaxation.

● **Water therapies** are an effective way of relaxing and are available in different forms. One of the most popular is the Jacuzzi; this bubbling tub full of hot water is a great way to warm your muscles. They are available at many health clubs and leisure centres, and you can also buy ones that are available for the bath tub at home. However, don't stay in too long – they can be dehydrating.

● **Flotation tanks** are now also widely available, the idea here being that you go into a small room or tunnel which is soundproofed, dark and full of warm water and Epsom salts. You lie in the water, and in this womb-like atmosphere you relax your mind and body. Of course, this doesn't suit everyone: some people find the water too cool while others may feel claustrophobic, but if you want to really block everything out for a while it could be a good therapy for you.

- **Other water therapies** include: cold packs (where the body is wrapped in wet blankets) and vivation (exercises in a birth pool).

- **Saunas, Turkish baths and steam sessions** can be very refreshing and relaxing. These methods involve sitting in a hot 'room', heating the body to a high but comfortable degree so that you relax tired muscles and mind and sweat out toxins from the skin. The Turkish bath and steam room use water or water-filled air, whereas the sauna environment produces dry heat. The sitz bath is also a great way of invigorating the body. This method involves sitting with your bottom in a bowl of water and your feet in a different bowl of water! The first bowl is filled with cold water and the second with hot water. After two minutes you swap bowls so that your pelvis is now covered with the hot water and your feet are now in the cold! This is surprisingly refreshing and dynamic!

Most water therapies are very relaxing as water is a natural and familiar substance, known to us even before our birth, so it makes sense that it can help to calm us. Water exercise, such as aquarobics or even just gentle swimming up and down your local pool, is a great de-stresser as it not only rests the mind but the water supports your body weight and can relieve aches and tensions.

Sleep

Sleep is probably the most fundamental relaxer of all. It allows the body and mind time to replenish their energy; it provides dream time for the mind to sort through the day's events; and muscles and ligaments relax because they are under no pressure.

Anybody deprived of sleep knows just how stressful and tension filled this can make the whole of the next day. If you have trouble getting to sleep, try some of the following ideas.

1 Internal massage

Imagine that two huge hands are placed over your skull. See them as they lie there, slowly penetrating through your head until they are resting on your brain. Imagine the fingers beginning to gently stroke and massage your brain. It is incredibly restful, and you can feel the layers of your brain releasing and letting go of all those hundreds of thoughts and calculations as it starts to relax. Imagine successive layers of your brain expanding and letting go of tensions as the magic hands caress and rub away your tension spots.

2 Unpeg your thoughts

If you have trouble getting to sleep because you cannot stop your mind teeming with thoughts, try this: imagine you are looking at a clothes line laden with clothes. This is all that fills your vision and you cannot see anything else. Think of each of your thoughts as an item of clothing on this line (it does not matter what the items are). Now picture the item of clothing being unpegged from the line, and, as it is unpegged, think to yourself, "Let go of the thought, put it away". The line of clothes is endless and with each item unpegged your thoughts are allowed to float away from your consciousness, and your mind will be free to drift into sleep.

3 Goodnight, it's time to get up!

Your mind may be telling you that you don't want to go to sleep – "Why should you? There's too much to think about and plan". Think about how you feel the next morning when you have to get up early. Think of that horrible day when you have to get out of bed and it's cold and wet outside and all you want to do is curl up and stay in the warm. Think of how you sometimes crave a lie-in.

So imagine that it's morning and that you have to get up but all you want to do is lie in bed and snooze. Allow yourself to realise that it's your day off! Suddenly all those things you had to get up and do have fallen away! You are free to sleep!

In conclusion

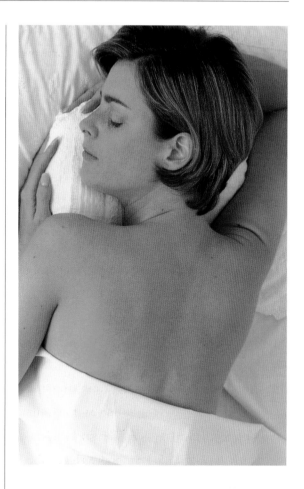

Individuals have differing sleep requirements – some get by on five hours a night. Sleep is so fundamental that you must ensure that you get what you need.

One of the best ways for finding a pathway into relaxation in your life is to listen to your body. Virtually all of the techniques and ideas expanded in this book involve working with the body in its most complete sense. That means working with the physical muscles and bones, working with the mind and working with the emotions, hopes, desires, dreams and innermost thoughts that make up our inner spirit. If you can get in touch with some of these aspects of yourself you can be sure you are approaching relaxation on a holistic level, which is the most beneficial way.

● When trying to integrate relaxation time into your life, always take a positive approach.

● Try not to complicate your life, keep it simple and don't make your relaxation sessions one more thing to worry about.

● Try to eat and sleep regularly.

● Finally, maintain your faith in yourself and your own powers. As long as you find time to relax and replenish them, they will grow and enrich your life.

Creating a stress-free day

WAKING UP

Once you have roused yourself from sleep, start the day really on top mentally, before you even get out of bed and start getting up.

● Sit up and say, "Where am I?" Make yourself look around and really see your surroundings for the first time! Notice things about your room you haven't noticed before.

● Think a new thought! Don't go back to thinking whatever it was you might have been worrying about the night before. Tell yourself today is a new day with new opportunities. Now get out of bed!

● Start the day with a healthy breakfast to revitalize your system. Drink fresh orange juice to refresh your palate and give you a boost of vitamin C.

Have some whole-grain cereal, which is high in fibre, and milk for energy, and finish off with a banana which contains potassium and is good for combating stress!

● Finally, before leaving the house, try running through the posture check (see page 54).

TRAVELLING TO WORK

Keep your posture well aligned as you sit in the car, bus or train on the way to work. Try to keep your spine erect and check that your shoulders are dropped away from the ears. As you start thinking about the day ahead of you and all the things you will have to do, check that you are not:

● Clenching your teeth

● Pulling at your nails

● Fidgeting

Make a conscious effort this morning to sit quietly and relax your body. Look out of the window and notice your surroundings. Take a deep breath as you mull over things that might challenge you in the day ahead, and repeat a positive mantra to yourself: "I will be able to cope with the day ahead. I will enjoy the day ahead." Remind yourself how you can bring relaxation to everyday tasks.

AT WORK

Today, nothing is going to get to you! Use some of the time management and decision-making suggestions in Chapter 4 to help you make better use of your work time. Don't forget to break your work load down into smaller tasks so that you can work through them, one at a time, and then tick them off as you finish them. Make sure you finish one job before starting another.

If someone or something starts to annoy you, use this as your cue to relax. Try to find a couple of minutes to take a deep breath. Picture the outwards breath as surrounding your body and enfolding you rather like a warm bath. Allow yourself to succumb to this feeling so that you calm down.

Why not cut down on your coffee consumption today? Try drinking eight to ten glasses of water instead. Keep a bottle of mineral water on your desk.

LUNCH

Eat a well-balanced meal for lunch. Opt for several slices of wholemeal bread together with a fresh salad, some lean meat or fish. Avoid mayonnaise and oily dressings, and finish with fruit and a cup of hot water. For more diet tips, turn to page 33.

If you are going out to lunch and are tempted to over-eat or to indulge in unhealthy foods, try the visualization for appetite control on page 35.

Try to go for a walk in your lunch hour. Walk fast, striding out with swinging arms to get the blood flowing. Or, if you can find a quiet space, try some yoga, dance or Tai Chi meditation.

Just before you go back to work, sit down quietly for two minutes and close your eyes. Let your thoughts drift past but do not follow them. Just let them cross your mind. Do not allow any problems to encroach on your consciousness; pull away from the issues of the day and just relax a little.

MID AFTERNOON

Are you feeling a little sluggish after lunch? Refer back to Chapter 4 to boost your powers of concentration and get more out of your afternoon.

EARLY EVENING

Find some time in your evening routine to do something relaxing. Let other chores take a back seat for this evening, and do what *you* want to do, whether it's decorating a room, reading a book or baking a cake. Small practical tasks can absorb the mind and body, and give relief from thinking about the day's events. Before you start, try some exercises to focus your creativity (see Chapter 4).

Try to concentrate intently on what you are doing. Each time you find your mind wandering, gently refocus on the task in hand. This will help to calm your mind. For other mind-calming ideas, try some of the meditation ideas in Chapter 5.

For a healthy evening meal, have some raw vegetables or salad together with some potatoes, rice or bread. End the meal with some fruit, stewed or raw. Treat yourself to a new herb tea – peppermint is very soothing.

GETTING READY FOR SLEEP

Towards the end of the day, a little exercise can help disperse excess energy so that you can sleep more easily without muscular aches or pains. Try performing a few of the gentle toners for the stomach and back (see page 55) or some mobility exercises (see pages 58-60). Next, have a long, warm bath and add some aromatherapy oils to the water to relax you. If you are feeling tense, why not have a massage, with your partner or a self-massage. Put on some soothing music before you stroke and knead your tensions away.

As you lay your head down to sleep, close your eyes and watch the darkness wash over you. Register your breathing for a while; listen to the sound of it and become aware of the breath entering and leaving your body. Finally, let your thoughts drift you slowly but gently towards a deep, reviving sleep.